Literary Voices
The Milford Series
POPULAR WRITERS OF TODAY
ISSN 0163-2469
Vol. 39

INTERVIEWS WITH...
BRITAIN'S ANGRY YOUNG MEN

Conducted by
Dale Salwak

BORGO PRESS / WILDSIDE PRESS

www.wildsidepress.com

To Myrtle C. Bachelder,
who helped make it possible

Library of Congress Cataloging in Publication Data:

Main entry under title:

Literary voices #2.

(The Milford series : popular writers of today ; v. 39)
1. Novelists, English—20th century—Interviews. 2. English literature—20th century—History and criticism—Addresses, essays, lectures. I. Salwak, Dale. II. Series. III. Title: "Angry young men."
PR106.L56   823'.914'09   81-21686
ISBN 0-89370-159-9 (cloth, $11.95)
ISBN 0-89370-259-5 (paper, $4.95)

Copyright © 1984 by Dale Salwak.
All rights reserved. No part of this book may be reproduced in any form without the expressed written consent of the publisher. Published by arrangement with the author.

First Edition——May, 1984

CONTENTS

Introduction, by Colin Wilson	5
I. Kingsley Amis: Mimic and Moralist	13
II. John Braine: The Man at the Top	41
III. Bill Hopkins: Looking for the Revolutionary	61
IV. John Wain: Man of Letters	67
V. Colin Wilson: The Man Behind *The Outsider*	82
Index	93

PHOTOGRAPHS

Dale Salwak and John Wain	4
Kingsley Amis	12
John Braine	42
Bill Hopkins	60
John Wain	68
Colin Wilson	93

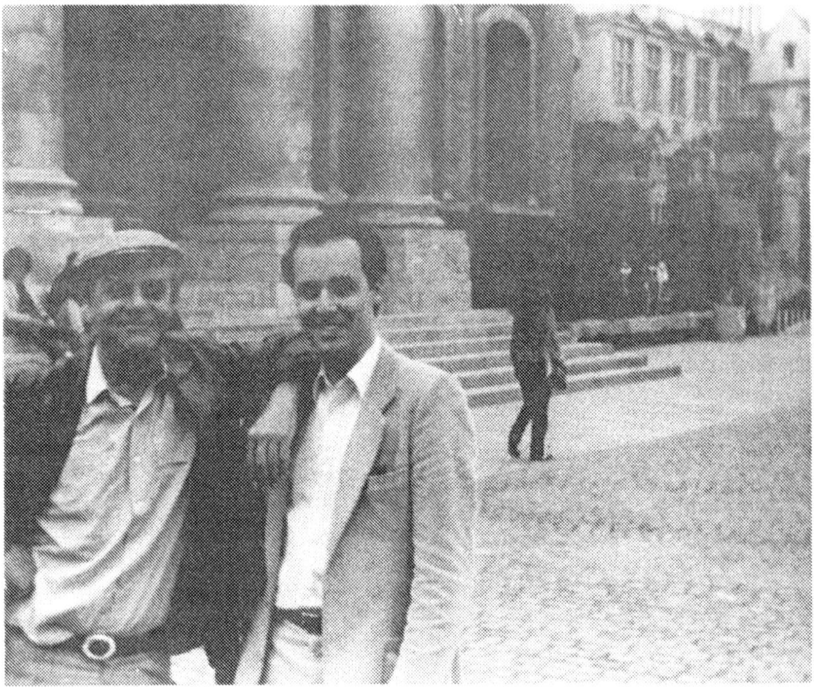

INTRODUCTION

When the first world war came to an end, the literary situation looked depressingly bleak. The famous writers who had made their names before the war—Shaw, Wells, Chesterton, Bennett, Henry James, Thomas Mann—now seemed old-fashioned, almost Victorian; but where were the new voices? By 1925, the hiatus was over, and the new generation—including Pound, Eliot, Joyce, Huxley and Hemingway—was busily engaged in the traditional sport of assassinating its elders. Twenty years later, at the end of the second world war, the literary critics scanned the horizon for a similar upsurge of literary talent. This time, nothing happened. Norman Mailer's *Naked and the Dead* was promising; but where were the others? In England, highbrow critics—like Cyril Connolly—got into the habit of remarking that the novel, as a literary form, was probably at the end of its life span. As the forties turned into the fifties, it looked as if they might well be right. There *were* a few interesting new talents—in England, the playwright Christopher Fry and the novelist Angus Wilson—but they were quite clearly traditionalists. What was expected—and what stubbornly failed to materialize—was a "movement."

It seems to be generally agreed that, as far as England was concerned, the "new generation" finally made its belated appearance in autumn of 1953, with the publication of John Wain's novel, *Hurry on Down*. It is a "picaresque" novel, whose slapstick humour seems to owe something to Smollett, about a young man who (as Wain says) "had been given the educational treatment and then pitchforked into the world" to find his place. He wanders from job to job, finding them all boring and dissatisfying. J. B. Priestley, whose own picaresque novels had been best sellers in the thirties, gave *Hurry on Down* an enthusiastic review; yet there was obviously a world of difference between Wain and Priestley. Priestley looked back nostalgically to the past, the old traditional values; Wain's attitude towards past and present was one of aggressive disgust.

But it was not until the appearance of Kingsley Amis's *Lucky Jim* in early 1954 that the critics took note of this new spirit of irreverence. Amis's humour is, on the whole, much more good-natured than Wain's; but the basic situation in *Lucky Jim* is much as in *Hurry on Down*: the bored young man, pitchforked into an "establishment" job as a university lecturer, finding the whole thing as irritating and boring as the writers of the twenties found their elders. Yet, on the whole, Lucky Jim does nothing particularly outrageous; his most rebellious escapade is to get drunk before delivering a public lecture, and to tell his audience that "Merrie England" never existed.

Iris Murdoch's first novel, *Under the Net*, came out towards the end of 1954, and critics decided that she completed the trio of rebellious young writers; her hero is even more rootless and purposeless than Wain's, a kind of literary hobo who drifts around London, drinking impressive quantities of booze and often sleeping rough. The question she is posing is obviously the same one that bothers Wain and Amis: what better *purpose* can the modern world offer the talented young? The Welfare State was already seven years old; and clearly, no one is going to quarrel with a society that does its best to provide its members with the basic necessities. But what about the total unfulfillment of the individual in this land of plenty, this society run by businessmen, civil servants and politicians? Iris Murdoch, who was also the author of a little book on Sartre, was clearly aware that she was asking the same king of questions as the existentialists; Kierkegaard said: "Force me into a system, and you negate me."

I first heard of Wain, Amis, and Murdoch when I was writing *The Outsider* in the British Museum Reading Room in 1955; a friend—Ian Willison—who ran the Department of Printed Books, told me all about them. Over the course of the next eighteen months, I looked into all three novels, but found little to interest me. I could sympathize with the rebellion of their heroes, but found their attitudes crude and simplistic. "Lucky" Jim Dixon talks about "filthy Mozart", makes a virtue of the fact that he never reads, and has a vague, general contempt for all intellectuals and artists. This kind of reaction against "cultured phonies" struck me as more depressing than the attitudes it hopes to deflate. The influences on my own work had been Eliot and Joyce, Sartre and Camus. And Sartre and Camus seemed at least to have taken a step beyond the disillusion of "the lost geneneration." But their negativity worried me: Sartre's assertion: "Man is a useless passion", Camus's belief that human existence is basically "absurd." How could such problems be solved except by *thinking*?

My *Outsider* was a kind of by-product of a novel called *Ritual in the Dark*, whose central theme was closely related to that of Amis, Wain and Murdoch. Its hero, living alone in his cheap room, feels alienated from modern society; yet he feels that the answer lies in a kind of mysticism. *The Outsider* was simply an attempt to spell out the issues more clearly, and to point out that they reach back to Goethe and early romanticism— to those "moments of vision" that made the romantics feel that life is infinitely meaningful, and to the despair they feel when the vision disappears. Schiller had stated the basic problem in *The Robbers*, when he makes his hero declare that true human greatness springs from freedom, not from the law; he then becomes the leader of a gang of robbers. De Sade had gone even further in his rejection of the law and society in the name of individual freedom. Yet becoming a criminal—no matter how attractive it may sound to a schoolboy—is no solution to the problem of how a man can gain his freedom; neither is selling your soul to the devil, the solution Goethe dramatized in *Faust*. The hero of *Ritual in the Dark* toys—at least in theory—with the criminal solution when he wonders whether a sex killer may not be expressing this same "existential revolt."

Although *The Outsider* was intended as no more than a pendant to *Ritual in the Dark*, it was finished long before *Ritual* was more than a collection of fragments. By a lucky chance, it was accepted by the first publisher I sent it to. It was published on May 25, 1956. It caused far more of a sensation than those first books of Amis, Wain and Murdoch, perhaps because it was launched by two enthusiastic reviews in Britain's two "intellectual" Sunday newspapers, and by a great deal of publicity about my working class origins, and the fact that I had slept out in a sleeping bag on Hampstead Heath. Within a few days of publication, I had appeared on radio and television, been photographed (in my sleeping bag) by *Life* magazine, and been interviewed by a dozen or so reporters. Suddenly, everybody was referring to any kind of misfit as an outsider.

It so happened that a week before *The Outsider* came out, a play called *Look Back in Anger* had been presented at the Royal Court Theatre. The English Stage Company had been formed by the poet and playwright Ronald Duncan and by the producer George Devine; they were united by a vague agreement that the English theatre was stagnating and that something new was needed. John Osborne was an unsuccessful actor whose *Look Back in Anger* was a long yell of protest about the general unsatisfactoriness of modern society and its destruction of individualism. The first night of the play had been unspectacular; the critics felt that it lacked plot, and that its hero protested too much. He rails almost solidly for three acts, denouncing everybody and everything—with particular attention to those members of the middle and upper classes that Amis had taken such exception to in *Lucky Jim*. But *Look Back in Anger* impressed one critic, another rebel named Kenneth Tynan, who roundly condemned the short-sightedness of his colleagues in a rave review in *The Observer*. This review appeared in the same issue of the newspaper that contained Philip Toynbee's review of *The Outsider*. Osborne and I became famous—or notorious—together. A few days later, J. B. Priestley discussed us both in a review in *The New Statesman* called "Angry Young Men." As far as I was concerned, the term was wholly inappropriate, I wasn't angry about anything, and had no particular views on the political or social situation. But the phrase stuck.

It was in the week following publication of *The Outsider* that the journalist Dan Farson took me to see *Look Back in Anger*. I found I disliked it even more than *Lucky Jim* and *Hurry on Down*. The hero seemed to me a self-pitying idiot, whose views were as unconstructive as Amis's. I have to confess—frankly, and with a degree of humility—that I have always had a total blind spot for Osborne. I have seen his most successful plays—*The Entertainer*, *Inadmissible Evidence*, and *Luther*—and simply found myself unable to take any interest in the situations they presented. (I should make a partial exception in the case of *Luther*, whose first half seems to me excellent; but then, like most of Osborne's work, it simply rambles on until it stops, with no conclusions reached.)

Suddenly, the critics decided that they at last had the "new generation" they had been waiting for. We were all Angry Young Men, including Iris Murdoch. The only other young writer on the horizon at that time was a young Jewish playwright called Michael Hastings; he was duly labelled Angry, although the general mood of his first play, *Don't Destroy Me*—dedicated to the memory of the late James Dean—is closer to distress. The newspapers were full of stories about Angry Young Men and Outsiders. We had arrived in time for the silly season—that lull in "hard news" that seems to occur most years in midsummer—and we seemed to provide some general ground for vague generalizations about social revolt. Within a few months, the journalists tired of their own creation, and decided to tear it to pieces. My second book *Religion and the Rebel* was slaughtered (*Time* magazine headed their review "Scrambled Egghead"), Osborne's musical *The World of Paul Slickey* was reviewed so contemptuously that it promptly folded, and new works by Amis, Wain and Hastings were discussed as if they were some kind of confidence trick.

By this time—say, late 1957—America had produced its own version of the Angry Young Man. Jack Kerouac was, in fact, older than any of us, and *On the Road* had been lying around in a drawer for some years before it was accepted; but when it appeared in 1957, it created the same king of sensation as *Look Back in Anger*, and, together with Ginsberg's poem *Howl*, became the manifesto of the Beat Generation.

In a sense, the Beat Generation was an artificial fabrication of the media, like the "AYMs." (The poet Kenneth Rexroth must also bear a fairly large share of responsibility—he seems to have invented the term.) But there was probably more sense in grouping together writers like Kerouac, Ginsberg, Rexroth, Clellon Holmes, Corso, Ferlinghetti, Snyder, and the rest than in linking writers with as little in common as Amis, Osborne, and myself. At all events, the Beat concept outlasted the Angry Young Men by quite a few years. In England, it was fairly clear by, say, 1958 that there never *had* been such a thing as an Angry Young Man "movement." All of them were now busily going off in their own directions, and the impression that they ever had much in common began to fade. Amis told one interviewer that he saw himself quite simply as a humourist, with more in common with P. G. Wodehouse than John Wain. Wain himself continued to practice the craft of the novel in a way that revealed he probably had more in common with Arnold Bennett—and other "observers of manners"—than with Amis. (I find him one of the most interesting of that generation, yet an underlying current of bitterness and aggressiveness in his work seems to me to rob it of the kind of vitality that Bennett could command.) Osborne's later plays seemed to reveal that his most characteristic mood is a kind of gloomy nostalgia for the past. His success has been based on a good ear for dialogue (which includes an impressive command of abuse), and a journalistic eye for topics of current interest. He is on record as saying that he wants to make people feel—which is no doubt why I find it hard to abandon myself to his work; I am inclined to try to make them think. John Braine—whose *Room at the Top* was the sensation of 1957—has always been basically a romantic, fascinated by sexual relationships. Reviewers of *Room at the Top* saw it as a novel about a ruthless young man determined to escape his working class origins. In fact, the hero never makes the slightest effort to get to the top; he just seduces the boss's daughter and marries her. Like Osborne, Braine has a deep underlying streak of pessimism.

Perhaps there might have been more sense in calling the "new hero" of Amis, Osborne, and the rest an "outsider"—or even "alienated young man." This certainly *was* what these heroes all had in common—from Iris Murdoch and Amis to Donleavy's Ginger Man and the characters of Pinter, Orton, and Stoppard. There was, in fact, a tendency to refer to the "new hero" as either an outsider *or* angry young man until about a month after *Look Back in Anger*; but the British press found anger easier to understand than alienation, and that settled it.

Most of the writers grouped together as "angries" had reason to regret it. By 1958, we were all in disfavour. My own books continued to get vitriolic or dismissive reviews for another ten years or so, which meant that I spent most of that time living off a bank overdraft. Osborne was lucky: he moved into film making, and successes like *Saturday Night and Sunday Morning* and *Tom Jones* brought him financial independence. Amis and Braine were also aided over the lean years by successful films of their books. Wain continued as a university lecturer, later a professor. Iris Murdoch—never angry, let alone a man—went on to develop a king of comedy of strange sexuality that indicates that, like Braine, she is basically a frustrated romantic. Others—like playwright Michael Hastings, or like my friends Bill Hopkins and Stuart Holroyd, had an altogether more difficult time of it; they had the misfortune to be grouped with the "angries" before their first books appeared, and the critics closed ranks, determined not to let any other young hopefuls clamber on to the bandwagon. All three became non-productive for more than a decade. Hastings and Holroyd have only just begun to re-emerge, while Hopkins' major novel (and play) about Christopher Marlowe looks as if it may take another five years to see the daylight.

A recent book on "the fifties" describes that period with nostalgia, as if it were already as legendary as the twenties. Possibly this is so, but I am no judge. I moved to a remote part of Cornwall in 1957, and have been here ever since. Reading these fascinating interviews gives me a feeling that it must all have been more interesting than I noticed at the time. But then, like most of the writers in this book, my real interest lies in the present and the future. The past is for literary historians.

Colin Wilson
Cornwall, England

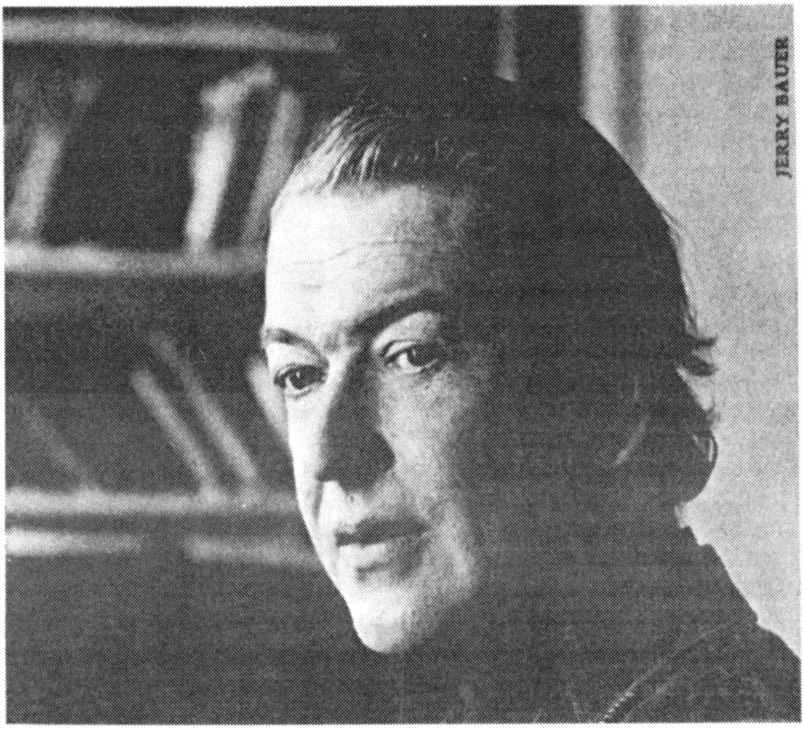
JERRY BAUER

I
Kingsley Amis:
Mimic and Moralist

Narrow streets swelled with shoppers in the noontime rush hour. Trains rumbled away from nearby Hampstead Station. Rain speckled the pavement of peaceful Flask Walk, and as I followed the housekeeper past a high brick wall, down some steep stairs, and into Gardnor House, the man who appeared in the extranceway was a man I had no difficulty in recognizing. I had written to Kingsley Amis before going to England about updating my past interview with him. With his never-failing courtesy he not only consented, but also invited me to lunch with him and his wife, novelist Elizabeth Jane Howard. And with his never-failing sense of humor, he had added: "We must arrange things so that you can't possibly mistake me for some relic of the previous generation."

Narrow stairs led into a spacious and book-lined sitting room. A small dog nipped at my heels. Ever able to produce the well-turned phrase for any occasion, Amis said, "She recognizes origins of distinction."

The room reflected its owners: cheerful, efficient, hospitable, unpretentious. Through lofty windows I looked onto a pleasant garden, which, together with the house, had the air of being obstinately self-contained. In the room, my attention was caught by shelves stocked with the thirty or more books Amis has written, many bound in black leather. The writings of some of his favorite authors lined the adjacent walls. Among them were books, handsome and otherwise, by Tennyson, Robert

Graves, Evelyn Waugh, Anthony Powell, H. G. Wells, and Graham Greene.

Moments later we were joined by his brother-in-law, Robert Howard, and by Amis' wife, a tall and imposing blonde lady. She settled comfortably in another chair, crossed her legs, and busied herself with needlepoint as we talked about dirigibles (an interest of Amis'), Howard Hughes' Spruce Goose ("Somehow that seems to have passed me by," said Amis), and raising children ("Not yet," I replied when Mr. Howard asked if I had any). Not very long afterwards Amis looked at his wife, his light blue eyes shining perceptibly brighter, and asked, "Well, where's this lunch you've been promising us?"

To get to the kitchen, we walked through his study, a fairly large room overlooking the side garden. The principle piece of furniture was a chair with a red sitting pillow and a plain wooden desk. On top of the desk were a bulky Adler typewriter, assorted papers, and five volumes of the collected writings of London journalist Peter Simple, for which Amis was writing the introduction.

Although it might be going a bit too far to describe the life that Amis and his wife lead as Edwardian, it does smack of an earlier, gentler era, and it is very English. Their eating habits are a case in point: the meal featured solid, dependable food, including water cress soup, lamp chops with mint sauce, roasted potatoes, salad, and red wine. Like my hosts, the housekeeper was the kind of person who knew exactly what she had time for. Although I tried, I could not catch her in the act of serving me. As in a well-orchestrated performance, food appeared before me like magic. My wine glass seemed to refill itself after every swallow. When faced with the decision of which dessert should come first, the cheese or the ice cream and apricots, the others deferred to the guest. "Let's save the cheese for last," I said. "Good!" Amis answered. "Then we can have more wine with the cheese."

In due course Amis and I were back in the sitting room. He was an easy man to question, and always forthcoming with his answers. He surprised me with a copy of his latest novel, *Russian Hide and Seek*, with the inscription: "A wet but cheerful afternoon, 14th July, 1980." And I caught a tantalizing glimpse of his famous talent for impersonations when he imitated a Soviet reviewer's attack on the novel. Then Mrs. Amis joined us and also signed her novel, *After Julius*, with the words: "This is Dale's copy of my book, which I inscribe with my very best wishes."

When Amis peered out the window, then leafed through a copy of the latest *London Magazine* "to find something to read," I understood that to be his polite way of saying that it was time to bid "Cheerio." Before parting, we made arrangements to meet one week later at his London club, the Garrick.

I. KINGSLEY AMIS, PART ONE

DS: Considering your background and education, did you find it particularly difficult breaking into the establishment as a young writer?

KA: No. I want to record an emphatic no to that one. I started off with no social advantage at all. I acquired two very substantial ones. Having been to Oxford and having gotten a good degree at Oxford helped a great deal. And I'd heard that there was a thing called the London literary racket which people used to talk about very much in the early 1950s, and that it was all an interlocking network in which Jones would review Smith's book favorably, and vice versa, in which jobs were given to people you'd been to school with, and so on. That may have been going on but I never saw it, and it never did me any harm. I found my progress unimpeded by any external matters of that sort. Perhaps people have been stabbing me in the back all the time without my noticing it. But it showed me that what I had thought when I was younger (in my teens and twenties)—the view that Britain is a very rigid, structured, separated society, and that it is very difficult to break through from once class to another—was quite untrue. In my youth, England was not very stratified and it's less so now. It's always been alleged that the English, particularly the English as distinct from the other British, have an upper-class accent and various kinds of inferior accents, but even that is going now. It would be very difficult at any rate for a non-expert to differentiate the way Princess Anne talks, for example, from somebody who is earning twenty pounds in a boutique.

DS: Looking back on your own career, can you reconstruct for me the way in which the "Angry Young Men" arose?

KA: As always, I think it was all certainly not one or two things. Rather, it was a combination of accidents. One was that it so happened that three or four writers (myself included), none of whom were from upper-class backgrounds or had been to public schools in the British sense, emerged at about the same time. And they were all roughly of an age, and it so happened that there had been a kind of delayed action effect after the war. John Wain appeared, it so happened, in 1953. I think there was a feeling of exhaustion after the war. The older writers were still writing, but for some reason no new writer of any fame, any note, had appeared for seven or eight years. I think this was partly because people were busy putting their lives together again.

I was twenty-three when the war ended, and I spent the next few years trying very hard to get a good degree at Oxford, overwhelmed by getting married, finding almost simultaneously there were suddenly two babies in the house, and getting a job and working hard at it. There was this lag of eight or ten years after the war when nothing happened. Then by a series of coincidences, within three years, John Wain appeared, I appeared, John Braine, John Osborne, Iris Murdoch, and Colin Wilson all appeared. And others. Now that looks like a movement, and I can quite see, since there was this business of non-upper-classness (middle-class, middle upper-class perhaps, but certainly not upper-class) people could be forgiven for mistaking this for a sort of minor revolution or turning point in English writing. I don't think it really was that, but it had the look of being one.

Another reason why the thing was made to look like a movement is the fact that the novels and the plays were to large extent about people at work. The hero of *Hurry on Down* wants to know where he fits in, where he's going to get a job, and changes his job a lot. The hero of *Lucky Jim* isn't sure what he wants to do, but we see him at work and a lot of his difficulties come directly from his job. Jimmy Porter in *Look Back in Anger* isn't employed very much but how he earns his living is important. *Room at the Top*, perhaps to a greater degree than any, is about a man getting on in the world. In other words, someone said that the weakness of the English novel of the twentieth century up to the time he was talking about (could be 1939) was that nothing happened until after 6:00 p.m. or on Saturday and Sunday. It wasn't that the people written about were of the leisure classes, it was just that we never saw them doing anything, apart from committing adultery and getting drunk. What they did at the office or at the factory, except for a few very self-consciously proletarian writers, we know nothing about.

DS: What are your feelings about the political novel? Norman Mailer has made a way of life out of this for the past ten years. George Orwell occasionally used the convention of the novel for political statements. Do you see any similarities between yourself and Orwell?

KA: I'd be flattered to think there were any similarities between myself and Orwell. I think that with the exception of *Animal Farm*, which is an incredible freak of nature—unique—I don't regard Orwell as much of a novelist at all. A fine writer and a man with marvelous ideas, but look at his novels. *Coming Up for Air* is absurd as a novel. *1984* has got some marvelous ideas, but no narrative pressure. You get one situation and then another situation and another, and that's about it. It's repetitive. You get it also in his best novel, *Burmese Days*, which is nearest to being a novel. A man is in a hopeless situation, meets a girl who he thinks is going to pull him out of his hopeless situation, and she lets him down. Same thing as in *1984*.

As regards Mailer, I think that's a wonderful example of self-ruination by going in for politics. When I read *The Naked and the Dead*, I thought, wow, look out chaps, here's somebody on the scale of Dickens or Eliot, better watch him closely. But I needn't have worried, because he's systematically destroyed his talent by being rather silly. Very intelligent man, brilliant gifts. He was a novelist in the very sense that Orwell isn't—he could narrate and develop. All this semi-political rubbish has made Mailer just a hollow shell. I can't read him anymore. This is what often happens to American writers; they cease to become writers and become institutions. Too successful, too much money, and something happens to them. There is so much temptation to become a national figure that you can become one, as has happened to Mailer and to James Baldwin (in a rather different way), although I don't think Baldwin had anything like Mailer's natural talent. Or you can disappear like Salinger, whose doom I lay squarely at the door of the *New Yorker* magazine for paying him the retainer. There are some people who flourish on being paid retainers because it stops them worrying about how they're going to pay for the groceries next week. Very few, however. I think most people need a little pressure like that.

DS: What is there to write about in England today?

KA: Anything. That question brings up the whole question of what the novelist is up to. And this brings up another thing which I think is in favor of the British writer here—he is not distracted from his proper task, which is to write about human nature, the permanent things in human nature. I could reel you off a list as long as your arm, beginning with ambition, sexual desire, vainglory, foolishness—there's quite enough there to keep people writing. Of course the terms in which these qualities express themselves must be contemporary, unless one's writing an historical novel, and I see nothing against that. If you say, for instance, I'm so interested in the anatomy of ambition or jealousy that I'm deliberately going to take it outside the present context, so there'll be no distraction, and I'm going to go back to the eighteenth century—there, nobody's going to say what a true comment on the present scene, because I don't want them doing that. I want them to concentrate on my subject. The dress in which these abstractions are clothed must be contemporary, unless the writer is detaching them deliberately, and the contemporary details must be right.

But it's not the job of the novelist to represent the contemporary scene in any sense. He may turn out to be doing that, if he's any good he may turn out to be portraying the contemporary scene, and perhaps later be a source for social historians, but that's not a thing you can try to do. If you try to do that you become either propagandist or trivial. Dickens, for instance, had certain things which he wanted to say about his contemporary scene, although most of that, the sort of social reforming element in Dickens, was a little bit behind the social clock. He would not take up a cause unless it had been pretty heartily taken up by the people in advance. What primarily interested him, I'm sure, was how extraordinary people are. What extraordinary things they can do and say when they are very hypocritical, when they're very respectable, and when they're very mean. And, incidentally, of course, he will show them being hypocritical and mean and so on in a contemporary fashion, wearing contemporary clothes in all possible senses of the term.

DS: Turning specifically to your novels, are you consciously aware of using comedy as a critical device?

KA: In a sense, yes. It's essential from my point of view that the bad people should be ridiculous as well as bad. In my novels there are good people and bad people, which is very rare these days. There's often a lot wrong with the good people, and one must also lay off by making the bad people say good things or be right about things that the good people are wrong about. There are bad people, and it is essential to make them ridiculous. So that Professor Welch [*Lucky Jim*], who is a bad person because he treats Dixon very badly, is ridiculous because it is essential that he should be. Bertrand is rather a bad person—pretentious, rides all over people's feelings, women's feelings especially. But he's also a ridiculous person. The bad people have got to be funny, so that's critical if you like. But then, of course, when it comes to the good people the thing becomes a little more complicated, and also the question of whether the good people are really good becomes complicated, too.

To make a good character prominent is very difficult. This has been a perennial, incurable problem ever since literature existed. I think that one would find in my books that it's much more likely that an important good character would be a woman rather than a man. I think that Jenny Bunn is a good character, and Patrick Standish is a bad character

[*Take a Girl Like You*]. He's in a way, I think, the most unpleasant person I've written about. I have sympathy for him, yes. He has his good points—when he pays for the other girl's abortion, for example. As a good character, Jenny is quite opposite to what Patrick could ever possibly be like, a good character who comes to grief and who has faults that one cannot get moral about. They are faults of foolishness, perhaps, indecision, but she is a person with wholly good instincts, generous, great humility, too much, really. There's also Julian, who is all that Patrick ought to be and isn't, because although immoral sexually, let's say (many people would disapprove of the way he conducts his life), Julian actually knows what one should do and what one can do and what one should not do. And it's Julian who denounces Patrick for his behavior.

Those are in a sense my two favorite types. One is the person who is naive and shrewd (Jenny), in other words inexperienced, sees things for what they are, would never be wrong about a person even though she might be taken in by some things about them. The other admirable person is the person who is like Julian, entirely his own man, not preyed upon by anxieties, guilts, doubts, but nevertheless, in fact, is sufficiently so that he can afford to behave morally. I mean by that, he would never have treated Jenny as Patrick did because he'd just have decided he had to leave her. He too might have been confronted by Simon [*I Want It Now*], but would have said, "Sorry, this is too much; there'll be another one along in a minute."

DS: In "A Memoir of My Father," you speak of the early training in morality you received. Could you elaborate?

KA: All the standard Protestant virtues (of course I know these overlap with Catholic virtues and Jewish virtues, and so on) were put forward and taken for granted—conscientiousness, thrift, hard work, patience, particularly. That is to say, one mustn't expect to run before one walks nor to be a success at anything to start with. Everything worth doing is going to take time and trouble, unstinting and unceasing trouble. These were very good lessons. But God never came into the conversation. God was never actually referred to or appealed to, and there was no question of displeasing God by my actions or trying to please him. My parents would take me to church on Armistice Day, sometimes at Christmas, but these visits got less and less frequent as they grew older. In the last ten, perhaps twenty years of their lives, they never went into a church. They had suffered, they said, from forceful religious indoctrination, being forced to go to chapel when young, and

I think my father regarded himself as a rebel in a mild way, mild certainly from today's standards. He had broken away from a very inflexible Christian kind of upbringing. When I saw my grandparents, they too seemed to have come out on the other side. God didn't come into the conversation much.

DS: Anthony Burgess, in his review of *I Want It Now*, comments that with the appearance of this novel a moral philosophy begins to emerge. How much stock do you put in a remark like that?

KA: Quite a lot. Again, I think it's improper perhaps to talk about one's self in such terms, but I've always been a moralist, which doesn't mean, of course, that I behave any better than anybody else. If I weren't a moralist I might behave even worse than I do in ordinary life. I think—and this goes back to dad and mom and so on, if you like—that because of my strong views that some kinds of behavior are admirable and others are despicable, hence I have this fairly rare phenomenon that there are good and bad characters. And very often they're not at the center of the stage, but minor characters who are completely good (Moti in *The Anti-Death League*, for instance) and completely bad (Dr. Best).

I think that it's become more obvious, if you like, that there's a moral concern at work. But I would have thought that it had been there from the start. If Jim is such a slime, why doesn't he tell Margaret to leave, as he could do. Admittedly they work in the same department and it would be awkward. Bertrand would have no trouble at all getting rid of Margaret. Jim hates it and at the same time laughs to himself about it, which is a thing some people miss; the only way he can bear it is by joking to himself about it. There is a responsible concern, and, if you like, at the end he says, well, there are limits and as a Catholic would say, the individual's duty is to save his own soul first.

DS: Do you see any time during your career when you have consciously modified the way you look at things?

KA: Yes, I think so. At any rate that's what it looks like. There's been an increase in the dim view which is taken of life, and the element of horseplay and high spirits decreases. But I'd say that I've always been a writer of serio-comedies, and I wouldn't be fair in ignoring the Margaret theme in *Lucky Jim*. I'm not claiming any merit for this, only trying to describe what it is—an attempt at studying a neurotic person who brings pressure to bear by being neurotic. It's true that Jim's response to this can be taken by the reader as amusing, as comic, but he doesn't think it's comic. He talks about it to himself, reflects about it. What he is trying to do is cheer himself up, to make it more bearable by trying to be funny about it. But that's quite a serious bit.

Even in *I Like It Here*, which has very little to say about anything, there are two fairly serious moral moments. One is when Bowen goes over to Strether's side, having regarded him first with uneasy contempt, and becomes protective. The incident which is supposed to show this is when he adjusts Strether's false teeth that had been half-knocked out of his mouth. The other thing is when he discovers something more about his wife than he thought, that she couldn't be a blackmailer's girl, something he'd never put to himself before, and that that was the most important thing about her.

DS: I notice that Jim Dixon makes a distinction between the "nice" and the "nasty" people, and that that distinction is referred to in your later novels. What does Jim mean by the "nice" life?

KA: That is an attacking rather than a propounding remark, against *nostalgie de la boue*. It's a critical remark, saying don't let's pretend that it's a good thing to starve in a garret, that the painful experiences are good for you, the disagreeable experiences are good for you. Let's just face the obvious truth that you're probably a better person and nicer to your fellows if you are reasonably contented, reasonably well off, and have a reasonably comfortable time. It's not a materialistic remark, nor is it a spiritual uplift remark, but it's an attacking remark.

Jim and I have taken a lot of stick and a lot of bad mouthing for being Philistine, aggressively Philistine, and saying, "Well, as long as I've got me blonde and me pint of beer and me packet of fags and me seat at the cinema, I'm all right." I don't think either of us would say that. It's nice to have a pretty girl with large breasts rather than some fearful woman who's going to talk to you about Ezra Pound and hasn't got large breasts and probably doesn't wash much. And better to have a pint of beer than to have to talk to your host about the burgundy you're drinking. And better to go to the pictures than go to see nonsensical art exhibitions that nobody's really going to enjoy. So it's appealing to common sense if you like, and it's a way of trying to denounce affectation.

DS: Jim also manages to emphasize the division of classes and is constantly reminded of his lowly status. Is this an exaggeration?

KA: He'd be the first to exaggerate it to himself, and I don't know how conscious I was of this at the time, but he's blaming his origins for things that his origins aren't to blame for. He's rather an uncouth person anyway; he could easily be more couth without his origins being changed. But I think that the proportion of that in *Lucky Jim*—the social climbing aspect—is not very important. For instance, Gore-Urquhart, who is Jim's eventual savior and benefactor, is certainly a man of the people who has made his way, but of heavy Scotch accent and therefore not one of the Scotch upper crust.

DS: In *That Uncertain Feeling*, an important question is raised when John Lewis turns down the promotion, presumably for reasons of integrity. However, Jean berates John for turning down the job and says economic security is more important. Is this ever resolved?

KA: I think that Lewis' scruples about turning down the promotion because it has been rigged are only half-scruples. I'm pretty sure if we could run the thing through again up to the point at which the promotion is offered, and Lewis had had a sudden burst of self-confidence, he'd say, "I'll take the money." What is at work is partly scruples, but not enough alone to make him act in a scrupulous way.

What is also at work then is an attack of sexual panic. Despite his views of himself—which are partly ironical, as a striding, sneering Don Juan—when he finds himself behaving like that he realizes that he hasn't got what it takes; he's afraid of getting really involved with Mrs. Gruffyd-Williams, and he's afraid of what this will do to his marriage. It's very largely a selfish fear which he then dresses up partly with scruples. But he uses them as a cover for his feelings of panic. He's in deep water, he's out of his depth, he's in a situation he can't handle. Then he strides in to Jean and says, "I'm a knight in shining armor, my integrity is at stake, I've turned down the promotion." He receives a well-earned kick in the stomach by Jean's obviously sensible retort, "What about the money? And what's so scrupulous about you in other fields?" That is a rebuke that Lewis has fully earned.

Some of Lewis' guilt feelings are sincere. He talks near the end about not giving up, not surrendering to one's desire for comfort, for sex, pleasing one's self all the time, and realizes that given his character, one can't hope to keep all those selfish desires in check all the time, but what he must not do is to stop trying to keep them in check, which means at least he won't be behaving badly all the time. This is, for him, a very realistic conclusion to come to.

DS: *Take a Girl Like You*, on the other hand, seems a little more complex.

KA: I began that in 1955, and put it aside to write *I Like It Here* because it was obvious that *Take a Girl Like You* was going to take a long time to write. I was already behind in a sense. I was very nervous after it. I started making notes for it in Portugal in 1955, then put it aside in 1956, and wrote *I Like It Here*, then took up *Take a Girl Like You* again. I was very nervous because it was going to be a new departure for me; I even made about twelve drafts of the first chapter. I compared the first with the latest, and realized the only difference was that the later draft was ten percent longer. So I went on with it at an increased rate.

People say, "I laughed like hell at your book," and in a sense this is the nicest anyone could say. But when somebody said to me about *Lucky Jim*, "Thank you for your serious book," I thought, "Ah, you see what I intended." When *Take a Girl Like You* came along, it was saying, to put it very crudely, I hope they'll go on laughing, but this time they won't be able to escape the notion that I'm saying something serious. I don't mean profound or earnest, but something serious.

DS: You speak of becoming grimmer in your view of life. Do you see any changes in values, in Jenny's speech at the end of *Take a Girl Like You*, for instance?

KA: That's meant to be a very sad moment, because in fact, compared to Standish's behavior, she's a better person than he is, and the Bible-class ideas are better than his, even though they are quite inadequate. This is her trouble—she is presented with a great moral imperative or prohibition, without being able to understand the reason for it, without being able to work out the reason for it, and without wanting it, without being temperamentally on the side of it. Although Jenny is working-class, this would not be the right term for the earlier heroes. I think Dixon would say indignantly, "What, working-class? I'm middle-class." I imagine Dixon's father as being a small shopkeeper, or a man in some commercial firm, a lowly position but still white-collar person, obviously lower strata. Lewis' father—I doubt if he ever went down into the mine—is probably an office worker.

The same sort of thing applies to Bowen. Jenny, however, had to be working-class, not for any kind of political or social reason, but purely for strategic literary reasons, in that she had to feel on arrival, and the reader must feel this, too, that she is out of her element altogether, and she feels that her element is inferior to the one that she's in. In fact, it's not, but she feels it. This has got to be emphasized by first a geographical shift—she has come south (things have gotten more mobile since 1958 in England, however). In those days for a working-class girl to come south was something of a step to take. Therefore, she is socially isolated; there's no one to go to see, everybody's a stranger, has advanced ideas, more money than she was accustomed to, and they all seem more glamorous than people at home, certainly. So she'd have to be working-class.

Also, since the book is about the bit of morality—what happens when people can't give any emotional backing to their beliefs—this wouldn't be plausible except from a working-class milieu where people are more backward in that respect. I'm expressing neither approval nor disapproval when I say backward—backward in a chronological sense. You'd certainly find people with that sort of morality in Wales during that period. But I'd just done Wales, so she had to come from somewhere else. I could have made her Scotch, but that would have raised other problems I didn't want. I already had a Scotchman in the story, and so forth. Northern England is a very varied place, but it is believable that in the smaller towns, in Yorkshire for example, a girl could have been like that, born in 1938 or so.

DS: Beginning with *Take a Girl Like You*, I notice more of an emphasis upon sex. In light of your review of *Portnoy's Complaint*, in which you said the novel was "unfunny," how do you feel about sex in the novel?

KA: Sex is a very important topic and most people are interested in it. I don't mean by that that it does no harm to one's sales; there is that, that is so. But it's also an immensely painful topic, and for that reason to laugh about it is important. This does not mean laughing *at* it, but its comic aspect is the only one one can hope to put into fiction. But to write about actual sex activity—what people do in bed, as opposed to people's sexual interests, schemes, seduction campaigns—except comically, I think, is impossible. I'd find it impossible. The moment I feel myself about to write a sentence which gives evidence of my sexual excitement, I stop. I don't much want to actually, but I would never do so because of how I feel when I feel that a writer is doing that to me. I become embarrassed. I've nothing against pornography provided it's well-presented as pornography, provided the writer says, "Look, you and I are going to have a jolly romp together, I'm going to tell you a story all about what people do in bed, and you're supposed to become sexually excited about it. Okay?" Fine. But if he says, "I'm telling you now a serious, also perhaps funny story, but anyway my aim is to entertain you and possibly to edify you," and if he starts trying to excite me sexually while he's doing that, it turns me off.

The other thing is if it's written about seriously, not pornographically but seriously—this is when I think the most embarrassment arrives. In some of the works of D. H. Lawrence, for example, there are serious attempts to portray a marvelous "fuck." I don't think it can be done. It's much funnier in its effect than anything I could possibly produce, but it also produces embarrassment. I don't mean sexual embarrassment, but the embarrassment one feels when one's heard something out of place, the wrong sort of thing is said.

Regarding the increase of sex, there is quite a lot in my novel, *The Riverside Villas Murder*, which is in part about an adolescent boy and the woman who lives next door. There's none at all in *Ending Up*. This is partly what a lot of writers do, their desire to elude categorization, to disappoint expectations. So I'm a funny writer, am I? This one, you'll have to admit, is quite serious. Oh, so I'm primarily a comic writer with some serious overtones and undertones? Try that with *The Anti-Death League* and see how that fits. So I'm a writer about society, twentieth-century man and our problems? Try that one on *The Green Man*. Except for one satirical portrait, that of the clergyman, it is about something quite different. So there is a lot of sex. Try that on *Ending Up*, in which sexual things are referred to, but they've all taken place in the past because of the five central characters, the youngest is seventy-one. So you dislike the youth of today, Mr. Amis, as in *Girl, 20*? Try that on *Ending Up*, where all the young people are sympathetic and all the old people are unsympathetic. This can be silly, but I think it helps to prevent one from repeating oneself, and Graves says the most dreadful thing in the world is that you're writing a book and you suddenly realize you're writing a book you've written before. Awful. I haven't quite done that yet, but it's certainly something to guard against.

DS: Roger in *One Fat Englishman* is certainly shown to be a ridiculous character, largely because he is taken out of his social element. However, near the end it seems you express sympathy for Roger. Is this part of your concern with treating all characters fairly, even the bad ones?

KA: One can't write about anybody that one hasn't got some sympathy for. One reviewer remarked that "Roger behaves badly in more different ways than is usual, even for an unsympathetic character in a novel, but I can't help feeling that the author likes the character, and so do I." Yes I do, I do feel a lot of sympathy for him because, I think, he's awful, all right, and he knows it, and this is no excuse. But it does point to a perennial human problem, I think, that I tried to pin down in Roger's character and experiences—that if one behaves badly, it's no help to realize it.

Roger is a bastard to a very large extent, and he understands it, and yet he can't be different. One isn't asking for sympathy for him exactly, but we all have our crosses to bear, and being a bastard and realizing it is a kind of cross which he bears. Right at the end, the author steps forward, so to speak, to sympathize with Roger, and Roger weeps because although nobody says so, he was actually in love with Helene, or loved her as much as he is capable of loving anybody, and now he's lost her. So yes, I sympathize with him, I invite the reader to, also, without condoning anything that he does.

DS: How did you feel about *The Egyptologists* after completing it?

KA: I've always enjoyed it. To fill you in, Robert Conquest wrote the original draft which had the idea in it, and most of the characters in it, and a lot of the dialogue, and the science fiction dream, the Nefertiti statue, and so forth. I put in the plot, I introduced the women, in fact, and the television debacle. But again, you see that horrible old morality keeps peeping up from time to time, when Schwartz falls in love with the treasurer, or starts to, and goes away. She sees that you can't run your life like that, it won't do for her, because it's a choice of what she is—she's either too starry-eyed about what life can be, or too decent and sensitive a person.

DS: Concerning Dixon's distinction between the "nice" and the "nasty," is Ronnie saying the same sort of thing in *I Want It Now* when he calls himself a "shit," or when Churchill in *The Anti-Death League* looks at the world and sees everyone as "nasty?"

KA: I think they overlap a bit, but I think that Churchill is voicing what Moti would call selfish self-indulgent *contemptus mundi*—why is the world so bad—as a way of making his (Churchill's) sufferings seem more important. I think that covers that remark, because Moti is not the voice of the author, exactly (how could he express the author's view totally, being an Indian with a totally different religious background). However, in that scene he is putting what the author would say when he says we must all try to become men.

As regards Ronnie, I think this is rather separate on the whole. He's making a remark purely about himself, and I think when he says he hasn't got the determination or the guts to be a full-time shit, to be a successful shit, I think this is perfectly true. It's like the man who doesn't sincerely want to be rich—he hasn't got the continuity of effort. In fact, Ronnie likes pleasure, and this is the thing about him from the start—at least I kept trying to introduce this notion. It's not a conscience at work. He has this habit of being efficient by saying what he thinks sometimes, a very bad practice if you want to be a success (never say what you think; rather, always think before you speak).

But Ronnie also likes pleasure, and he likes women, and this is emphasized several times, and power seekers, in my experience, don't like women. They may sleep with a lot of them, but that's a different matter altogether. And almost at once he starts liking Simon (much later he realizes he can't do without her). If he wasn't capable of liking her, none of it would have happened. He'd have said, "Oh the hell with this, this is too much trouble. I'll find someone else." Obviously there's something wrong with that book, because a lot of people said they find that Ronnie's sudden conversion is unconvincing and suddenly he starts behaving well. I thought that it was unconvincing because it was so obvious that that's what he'd do, because the early part of the novel is full of pointers in that direction.

DS: How seriously then should we taken Ronnie's conversion at the end?

KA: I don't think it's a conversion. Rather, it's the plot that comes into importance here. If things had been different (what we say about any drama or literature), none of this would have happened. As Milton says—to compare the great things to the small—if Othello had sacked Iago in Act I of *Othello*, Othello and Desdemona would have got on perfectly well for the rest of their lives. That's a grand example, but I give it because it's such a well-known one. If Ronnie had been different, he wouldn't have bothered with Simon at all. Right from the start of their relationship he is concerned with her, before he knows that she is rich, and this is very important.

The turning point in the novel comes far too early from my point of view. He sees her at the party, he likes her, tries to take her on, is separated, she reappears in the street without any shoes and such, he tells her to clear off, she says she has no money. He then says he has to do something about this girl, and after they've been to bed (unsuccessful as it is), before he finds out that she has money, he's very angry when she won't go but is also concerned, I think. It's not as if a last minute Dickensian change of heart occurred, where Scrooge suddenly says, "Come on, let's bring out the turkey and the plum pudding and let's all be generous to each other." I would like to think that it's there from the start.

DS: I notice that your novels often conclude with the two central characters turning to each other for support: John Lewis and Jean, Ronnie and Simon, and Churchill and Catharine, for instance. Is this intentional, or did it just work out that way?

KA: I hadn't really considered the point before. Perhaps it happens to work out that way. Two going off together is a very common ending for all sorts of movies and books and so on, and perhaps that had its influence on it. But I suppose it's a rather sentimental feeling, if you like. Among all the disasters that have taken place and all the people that have been disappointed, these two have at any rate got each other, which is some sort of consolation. Also, if you like, the idea that one can't be happy on one's own, you can only be happy with another person, and so I suppose in a sense I am saying that by these endings.

DS: How earnestly should we take the supernatural in *The Green Man*?

KA: As earnestly as possible, I would say. It all really happens; none of what is recounted happens only in the hero's mind. It's all literal in that sense. I think we can fit the supernatural part into the natural part by saying that the hero is made aware of his own deficiencies by finding out that the reason he's being picked on by the dead wizard to fulfill his designs is that the wizard feels Allington's character is essential for the wizard's purposes. Allington being a man who doesn't care for people and manipulates them for his pleasure. That's the link between them. I think it should be taken very seriously; I took it very seriously. And naturally I enjoyed doing it, and brought in some devices that had been in my head for years. I'd always been interested in the supernatural in fiction; here was a chance to do a ghost story.

As always, when you start to construct with plot it turns into something else, such that the ideas about the supernatural that you had in the past seemed to have somehow produced ideas in the natural world that fit in with them. I'm a very firm believer in the idea that the unconscious does two-thirds of the work. For example, the idea about opening the window and seeing it is light inside and yet dark outside, and the idea that everything stops outside, and that you can't move, can't leave the room because you can't get through the air molecules (it's like concrete). That too had been in my head somewhere. The idea that it is dark outside became an obvious link in the chain of supernatural circumstances. And the idea that everything stopped outside became attached to the idea of God or His emissary putting in an appearance. In what other way could God visit a mortal human being except by making everything stop outside? Otherwise, somebody might come in and we can't have that. It's God's security measure that makes everything stop, if you like.

DS: Is your portrayal of God in *The Anti-Death League* different from the being in *The Green Man*?

KA: These are two very different incarnations. In *The Anti-Death League*, it isn't an incarnation at all in a sense. This is a view of the malignant God, who is very well described in Empson's *Milton's God* where he states practically, I think, that the orthodox God of Christianity is very wicked, and gives reasons for this. He sees God playing in *Paradise Lost* not altogether a dissimilar role from the role God plays in *The Anti-Death League* (although, of course, Empson's book was written before my novel ever appeared). I think if you were to look at that, this would throw some light on *The Anti-Death League*. In the novel, God is showing his malicious, malevolent side.

The Green Man takes a rather different view, and I'm not sure if they are really reconcilable. *The Green Man*'s God is slightly malignant, doesn't at all object to inflicting suffering, but that is not his main concern. He's running a game that's much more complex than that. He's admitting that he's not omnipotent, and that what may strike Allington as very arbitrary is in fact forced upon him because of the rules of the game. The chap in *The Green Man* does get tempted occasionally (let's throw down one dinosaur into Picadilly Circus and see what will happen), and that's the sort of thing with the being in *The Anti-Death League* (let's give her a cancer, smarten them up a bit; so that priest thinks he's in communication with me, does he—all right, let's sort out his dog). Of course I incarnated God in *The Green Man* as a young man simply because he can't be an old man with an enormous white beard. The idea of a young, well-dressed, sort of aftershave lotion kind of man, I think, made him more sinister. That was the intention, anyway.

DS: Turning away from fiction for a moment, what do you find satisfying in the writing of poetry?

KA: It's a higher art, and there's still even today a certain, almost mystical status which attaches itself to a poet which the prose writer hasn't got. Many of us would be poets full time if we could, but we can't. Auden could do it, although he wrote a lot of interesting prose as well. If one's mainly writing fiction, one would think that all one's creative energy goes into creating fiction. Some subjects, however, are not suitable for fiction. I'm delighted when I can write a poem.

There are several compensations for growing older as a writer, as you get to know yourself better, in your writing inclinations, and so on.

One gets more cunning, improves one's technique slightly as one gets older. You realize you get a little bit better at making transitions, such as realizing what a handy word "later" is (saying, for example, "What a marvelous old chap that fellow was," Roger said to Bill, later—thus eliminating the need for describing the end of the party, the departure of guests, and so on). You come to identify more precisely when to start a novel, and this is again not a conscious thing. It suddenly dawns on you that you know enough about your characters to start, and you understand your central situation to start. That means a certain amount of what you are going to say is already arranged in your mind. The same applies to political journalism, for example. Having written the first sentence, one ought to be able to take a rest, because one has done half the work. The great besetting fear is finding yourself with nothing left to say. I've tried to hedge by trying to write different sorts of books, partly because I like ghost stories, detective stories, spy stories. *The Riverside Villas Murder* is a detective story, set in 1936 in the middle of the great period of detective stories. *Ending Up* is very orthodox.

2. KINGSLEY AMIS PART TWO

DS: *The Riverside Villas Murder* seems to indicate your preference for genre fiction over the mainstream novel. How would you respond to that?

KA: Well, it's obviously a vital question, yes. I like to keep a foot in both camps. As long as I can, I'll go on turning out novels about society in England, now or recently. But it becomes harder, there's no question about that. The number of what I call straight novels for that purpose that anybody has in him is limited. And as one grows older it's increasingly difficult to say what's going on. I know what's going on around me, but nowadays, if somebody were to ask the question what's happening in London, my son Martin is the person to ask that. I'm jolly good at what's happening in the Garrick Club. I might even tell you something of what's happening politically—perhaps more than I'd be able to do thirty years ago. But perhaps the faculty of recording, of observing the life around one—and it gets worse with age—gets harder and harder to apply. So genre fiction is an attraction. I can cover myself a little by saying I've always done that. *I Like It Here* in 1958 was partly a travel book. More recently, *The Anti-Death League* was partly an espionage story. But I can't disguise the fact that the genres have taken more and more of my attention.

In my collected short stories, on the contents page I intended to put a gap between the titles halfway through. North of the gap is straight fiction. South of the gap is genre fiction. "The House on the Headland," for example, is a horror story masquerading as a secret service story, set in 1899. The narrative starts in 1939 and flashes back to 1899. "To See the Sun" is a vampire story set in 1925. It's in the epistolary convention. So yes, that proves it or shows it.

DS: In your vampire story—"To See the Sun"—you invite the reader to sympathize with the creature?

KA: Yes. I delivered the collected stories to my publisher. Before he had read the vampire story, he said in the course of a conversation: "Do you know there's a new kind of genre in fiction being written? It's called weepy creepies." He said it takes some monstrous kind of creature—like Frankenstein's monster, a werewolf, a mummy, I suppose, or a vampire—and invites us to sympathize with that creature and look at matters from his point of view. Well, "To See the Sun" is a weepy creepy because the heroine is a vampire who falls in love with her prospective victim and destroys herself walking out into the sunlight. I had a lot of fun doing that because it involves research of a sort. The story is set in 1925—you can imagine a real vampire surviving until that age, when communications must have been worse, far worse than they are now. So I had fun inventing a language. It can't take place in any real place—no fun in that—so it takes place in Dacia, which used to be a location during the Romans and is where Romania is now. Also, ergot. This is a fungus that grows on rye and produces hallucinations. There were a lot of outbreaks of that in the 18th and 19th centuries. And those hallucinations are very communicable. It's amazing what you can find in an encyclopedia.

DS: Although *Ending Up*, your next novel, is a rather bleak work, should one necessarily take it as your final word on the subjects of old age, the future, and so forth?

KA: Not really. There are two things. One is that you can say—quite an important point in the understanding of fiction—that no novel or poem is ever anybody's last word on any subject, nor is it a settled view that one has. The example I often take—an imaginary example—is to say how little a novel says about its author's life or what the author thinks or feels about his life. If someone were to say to Kipling at a relevant time, "I see you're leaving your wife, Rudy." "Why do you say that?" "Oh, well, it says here, 'the female of the species is more deadly than the male, and he travels the fastest who travels alone.' Surely that means if those are the views you hold, you're off." And he would say, "I feel like that occasionally and with luck those are thoughts that everybody thinks occasionally." So these become parts of a poem because those are thoughts that everybody thinks from time to time, but people don't run their lives on that principle as a rule.

Well, that's the end of point one. Point two: yes, that's all very well, but here you are writing a whole book about this, so it's more than a passing mood. It must be a recurring mood. So the reader or critic has got to pitch his understanding in the middle between these. He mustn't think it's the author's program—how he runs his life, or how his feelings are in any settled way. He'd be foolish to suppose and it can't be true, can it, that, judging from *Ending Up*, for most of the time I think old age is marvelous and dying is something to look forward to with positive anticipation and even equanimity. So bleak, you say. Well, I think people get bleak.

DS: Can you say something about the inspiration or starting point for *Ending Up*?

KA: Yeah, and as you said before, I think, sometimes the starting points are very obscure. Even the author, above all the author, just can't remember how he came to think of it. In other cases, of which *Ending Up* is one, it's quite clear. In this case there were five of us of different ages all living in the same house, the one in Barnet. My mother-in-law, then approaching eighty, I think; my wife and myself; her rather younger brother; and a friend who was residing with us for several years. I'd just thought one day, well, what happens when we are all very old, or pretty old. Then of course I saw at once that that really wasn't going to happen, because we were all of different ages. My mother-in-law was going to kick off before the rest of us, and indeed she did.

But then I had the idea of five people. It turned out to be five—five in life and five in the book, probably a coincidence. But it is a good number, isn't it? If you have nine old people it becomes a bit crowded. The author is spreading himself thin. If you have three old people, it's a bit dull for the reader. You've then got to go very heavily into the relations between the three. So five seemed about right—in an isolated environment which would suit old people. When I say "suit," I mean that most old people these days of the middle classes are fairly impoverished. So they'd have to live somewhere cheap and wouldn't be able to get about much. And you'd have all the advantages of a closed environment, but not as closed, as say, a ship or a prison, because there'd be quite frequent contacts with the outside world. And also, the other observation which is not a very special one is the intensification of character as people get older. If they're rather short-tempered in their youth, they'll be very short-tempered in their old age. Other things like that, and that was my start.

DS: *The Alteration* is by far one of the most ambitious books you have written. Would you say that?

KA: Yes, it was. That was one of those cases when I felt it was forced on me. With that I can say that I had a strange compulsion to write it more than almost anything of mine I can remember. And it was crystal clear how that arrived in my life. EMI, the gramophone company, issued an album to commemorate their 75th anniversary. This was in 1973, I think, so you had 75 years of their records or extracts of records. One of these was made in 1909 by a chap called Alessandro Moreschi, a *castrato* singer. I thought they were all gone. I thought they all belonged to the 18th century. No, Moreschi died in 1922, the year I was born. He had a very successful career as a singer and as director of the Sistine choir. Alistair Cooke introduced this record of his, but through no fault of his made it impossible to play it more than once or twice. He said, "Now get yourself ready for a very strange noise." The strange noise began, and it was this *castrato* singing the old *Ave Maria*. I like to think that I'm sensitive to music, but not that sensitive. All the same, I found it an intolerable noise. From a musicianly point of view it was very good as far as I could tell. He hit all the notes in the middle. The tune gets up quite high at the end, and he hit those in the middle, too. I thought, my God, this strange creature. Think of all he had given up and also all that he had gained as well. And instantly I thought I'll never play that record again. But I must do something to try to get it out of my mind. And I realized that on one side you had lined up sex, family, love, and the sense of living life with other people; and on the other side you had fame, money, success, art, and duty to God, to name a few. That's a fairly powerful line-up. It was with reluctance that I took it on. These are grand themes, but there's no way to evade them if the book is going to be written at all.

So by that fact, of course—the fact that we're dealing with a *castrato*—this determined everything about the novel. I spent some weeks saying to myself, "I can't face all that research on 18th century Italy, or indeed, of course, Spain." I thought we might have the coward's way out or John Fowles' solution—to put it all on a Mediterranean island. It occurred to me that I'd been saying to myself on and off for a long time, it'd be fun to write some science fiction one day. So the thing was clear what I'd have to do. It'd have to be in the present, 1976. But an altered present. Then it became clear that we'd have to have some sort of an authoritarian state; since it was a Catholic one, then the most powerful man in the world was the Pope, and so on. And so the hero has got to go to Rome, because if a story about the Catholic world doesn't include a visit to Rome, it is no good. Why? Well, obviously because the Pope is head of it. So, a great deal was determined from the beginning. But I found that as these things do happen—this is the textbook case—if you set out with your moral, if you say, for example, that I'm going to write a novel to prove, or to suggest strongly, that women shouldn't ever have been given the vote—then you're very unlikely to produce anything reasonable. You find out what your moral is while you are writing.

In this case I found out what it was after I'd finished the book. Of course, it has nothing to do with art or with sex, but it's a gloomy message about mankind, really. No matter what you do, how you set things up, you'll end up with a lot of oppression, and there can be times and places where there isn't much oppression, like England and the United States at present, but perhaps the characteristic or inevitable tradition of man is to impose some sort of oppressive state or other. It's not necessarily overtly political, but by one way or another the means will be found for making life unpleasant for people in one way or another. I didn't know I was saying that when I started.

DS: With *Jake's Thing* in mind, what in your view is the chief distinction between fiction and the real world?

KA: Oh, how much tape have you got? Well, I suggested one already, that I think is a very fundamental point. You can only suggest in the novel a part of the real world. That's obvious enough. I mean that the novel is ridiculously simplified compared to real life, using tricks that wouldn't or shouldn't be allowed in any journalistic report. You don't just heighten contrast for purpose of emphasis. You don't just quote selectively, leaving out things that don't suit your argument, as you might expect in journalism. You invent evidence in order to prove your point, if you have a point. There's also this matter of presenting views of one's world, sometimes rather fleeting views derived from a passing mood, and turning them into a law of existence. So a novel can't say women are oppressed in a lot of places or sometimes, but there are of course 500 million exceptions to that which I'm going to tell you about with equal emphasis. It's got to say women are oppressed, and give a handful of exceptions to show that you're not mad and not taking a changeless view of the world. Or it's got to say women aren't oppressed at all with admittedly some exceptions. It simplifies and it distorts and it substitutes fixity for change. That's a concept of the novel, but my view of that may be rather different next time. It's final by mere fact that it's a novel and published.

The other thing—apart from theme and event—is character. Any fictional character, even very complicated ones like Shakespeare's, is grossly oversimplified when compared with any real person. I don't think this matters very much. But it means that characters are moods, too, following the novelist's mood, obviously. So Jake in *Jake's Thing* is somebody who feels all the time the way I feel some of the time. But so do them all, all those heroes of mine. It's not so much that I'm such a varied or complex person, but a small bit of yourself is quite enough to use as a basis for a fictional character. Otherwise, the novel would be impossibly long or certainly hard to follow. It would lack direction, wouldn't it?

DS: Would you say that your selection of poems for *The Oxford Book of Light Verse* in any way reflects on your own poetry? Is your right-hand critical sense, as it were, completely divorced from your left-hand creative sense?

KA: I think they go very much together. And because starting off to write, starting off to be a poet, my sort of poet anyway, you start by admiring certain things, preferring some poets over others, which is not a thing that everybody does. There's a thing called breadth of field or breadth of taste or something, whereby you can admire Philip Larkin and also have a lot of time for Ezra Pound. My view is that if you really admire Larkin, and really understand him, you can't have any time for Pound. You can produce other pairs I'm sure. So, you sort of have strong likes and dislikes. And then in time it seems to be possible to produce more of the same, with luck, so the same that I would produce more of would naturally be very much the kind of thing I like. So that I think is an instant link between the critical sense which is, if you like, just being articulate about one's preferences and the creative ones, if it's that. There are bound to be resemblances there.

DS: I notice that a great many English writers seem to disappear from London, seem to be more out of England than in it. Graham Greene, for example, who traveled to Viet Nam, Haiti, Mexico, Cuba, and elsewhere; W. Somerset Maugham, or even Evelyn Waugh. Why do you think this is? Does it at all tempt you? Any regrets about staying in England?

KA: Well, I think probably there are different reasons at work here. Graham Greene is a very peculiar kind of writer, really. He hasn't been much about this country, as you say. He certainly hasn't lived here much of his life. I don't know why he does that. There's a tradition of doing that. Maugham was always on the move to the Far East and United States and parts of Europe, as well. In his case he had—it sounds absurd to say about a man who wrote so much in fiction and drama—weak pressure of his own invention. I mean that, if he sat in London, not much would occur to him. He wouldn't hear much and people wouldn't tell him things or would tell him things he knew already or had heard about. In a hotel in Singapore he might hear something very striking, new to him and also new to his potential readers. And he was restless, had to keep moving, and to keep his ideas coming. Same was true of Evelyn Waugh, who I think was a man haunted by the prospect of drying up, and who would say, "I've got to be off, I must get out of England. I must get out of London." He'd got to South America or Africa on purpose—for new sights and new stories. Perhaps I should be traveling too, in light of my earlier remarks about finding it more difficult to see what's going on. But then by temperament I'm so strongly a non-traveler, and more and more I've come to feel comfortable around London and in my own house. I've got my club and various other places. Going around England a bit—there are places in England to see. But I'm not the kind of chap who is going to live abroad or ever visit abroad very much. I think this may be a weakness or a source of weakness, and of course one pays dire financial penalties for staying here. But against that I feel that, if it's less easy to notice what's happening in my surroundings when I know the surroundings very well, it's certainly going to be harder abroad, isn't it, when visiting a new place. I'll be shocked by obvious differences, and I don't think novelists deal with obvious differences very much. I think it's more differences you don't expect. That's my sort of novelist. Differences that seem to be no differences, but on investigation and reflection turn out to be differences. For every gain there is a loss, so to speak.

DS: It seems that American writers are still relentless in following the self-conscious arguments of modernism. Barth's *Letters*, for example, in which he repeatedly calls attention to the artiness, the artificiality of it all. Are such writers working an outworn tradition? Does anything come of this artificiality?

KA: Oh, I see no point in that at all. I mean that this seems not progress, which is a very questionable idea anyway, but a regression. They were wondering in Sir Philip Sidney's time about that and saying, "Well, look, the poet is a liar. All this is untrue. How dare you tell these lies." And then Sidney had to say, "the poet lieth not for that he affirmeth nothing." I think people ought to abandon that and say "Yes, of course it's artificial." I think it shows a loss of confidence when people question what was rightly taken for granted. But I don't think any critical theory or theory of creative work—because it starts giving him other reasons for doing what he is doing. Philip Larkin remarked to the effect that a poet, for example, if he has a critical theory, will produce poems and naturally try to square with that theory instead of write the poems that only he can write. So like Larkin, I make a point of not having any theory of literature.

One added point to what I said earlier about the relationship between life and fiction: life and literature all arise out of the fact that life has no meaning, but literature has meaning, the novel has meaning. By using one as material for the other, the novelist is already making a tremendous step. But it shouldn't bother him if that is what he's doing. That's what he's always done. It's good that occasionally a writer says, "Look, that's artificial, that's not what life is like. I'm just trying to record it more faithfully." Until recently, revolutions were all in the name of fidelity to fact. It's not like that, it's like this. And from one generation to the next it used to be like that, but this is what we have now. There are various incompatibilities between literature and life, and there always have been. They stare us in the face. And one could go on defining and refining them, but to say that this suggests the whole system needs an overhaul is wrong.

DS: A lot of readers look to novelists for entertainment, much as they watch television or go to the movies. Is that how you see yourself, as an entertainer?

KA: Well, first, yes. Historically first, that's what I wanted to do. But I think it should be. I think that every novelist ought to entertain before he does anything else. And that's very difficult. It's much easier to be serious and to seem important, or to seem serious rather than to entertain. That is the hardest thing in the world, and just because some people do it with facility is not to say it is not hard. Being funny, for example. P. G. Wodehouse was funny. Since he wrote so much, it seems he did it without trying, without effort. But to say that is to mistake result of effort, of application, for really doing something. He said he always found writing very hard. I can't believe it, from looking at the result. It's effortless in the way that somebody playing the violin is effortless; in other words, not at all effortless. He just makes it look easy.

I like to be entertained with what I read. I might say, parenthetically, that a lot of novelists on being interviewed or in talking about their novels forget that they're readers and that they spend more of their lives being readers than writers. I find the number of people who have entertained me very small. And it's a very hard thing to convince people that this is something that has to be worked at. Part of that, of course, is being readable. You want to find out where the story does lead. Well, that's something that's got to be worked out too. There is something that has always stuck in my mind. When *I Like It Here* was published and it didn't get a good press at all, one chap said, "Mr. Amis is as readable as ever—that fairy's gift does not desert him." Patience really is what makes you readable. Patience on the writer's part, and that's something that's in short supply. It's getting in a shorter supply. So with poetry. A poem is not something that can be dashed off, though more and more people think it is. A poet has got to be readable, too. Just like readers of novels, we expect of our poets that they should be readable. In other words, they should have incredible persistence to stay with revising and re-revising their poems until they're in their best possible form. And again, I think in its way poetry has got to be as readable as fiction, along with the other things that it's trying to be and to do.

DS: How did the idea for your latest novel, *Russian Hide and Seek*, come about?

KA: Well the way that grew up is really quite straightforward. On Sunday morning I was looking out onto this garden, and I heard myself say, "They're not here yet, Ivan." Meaning—well I didn't quite know what I did mean. One day perhaps there'll be Russians in that house. And at a later stage I stayed at a very grand house in Northamptonshire. I found myself saying the same thing. I found myself thinking, "Ah yes, this is exactly where he would be. This is the house where the Russian Regional Controller would live." And a lot of things immediately followed from that. I was a little scared of it at first. But it seemed to be too much fun to be resisted.

This novel is a great remove from what we see. In other words, it's not our world. In this case it's fifty-five years in the future. If you can tie it down to some local bit of reality, that's good. So the house in the novel is the house I know. And so there are a lot of other real places.

The town of Northampton, the town hall, and so on. Which of course is the headquarters of the Russian security forces. But it's about the present society, too. I did know a bit about this in advance, so perhaps it's a weaker novel; that is, I knew what I was talking about even while I was doing it. But it shows the results of the collapse of all beliefs or ideas about how you ought to behave. All religion, of course, is long gone. Belief in Marxism is gone, too. Belief in what might be called a civilizing mission on the part of the Soviets is gone, if it ever existed. None of the characters have any reason beyond whim and what they've read to behave as they do at any moment. That point I didn't quite realize I was saying until I got to the end of it. Meaningful behavior, morally meaningful behavior, depends on there being some sort of structure. No system of beliefs exists by which society can judge somebody and by which somebody can judge himself. When your only interest is in surviving life becomes meaningless and not worth living.

DS: I understand you also wrote a novel, still unpublished, during the early 1940s while attending Oxford. Can you tell me something about it?

KA: It's not really interesting. A novel that I'd admired enormously, and which is quite unknown (an English novel), called *The Senior Commoner*—about life at Eton—made a tremendous impression on me. It's one of those curious novels in which absolutely nothing happens at all. Smith goes to see Jones and they talk, and then Jones goes away and runs into Brown and then Brown goes away and runs into Smith. It's about school life with no story to it.

I fell under the lure of this. There is a very crude and absurd story in my novel, called *The Legacy*, which again has a moral line in that it starts off with a young man who has inherited some money on conditions that he enter the family business (which is frightfully dull—accounting or something), and marries the girl his elder brother approves of by a certain time. He wants to be a poet and he has a nice girl, but by the end says to hell with poetry and marries the nasty girl and that's all that happens. I suppose there are some mildly amusing bits of observation, when he goes to live in a boarding house for a time and the people in the boarding house are studied. It's really no good and not funny.

DS: John Gross wrote a fascinating book entitled *The Rise and Fall of the Man of Letters*. How do you feel about being classified as a man of letters?

KA: To him the man of letters is the man who gets most of his income from journalism and writing memoirs of people, collecting their letters, and all that type of stuff. I think that for me nothing really important had taken place since about 1880, in the sense that while lots of interesting books have been published, I think of myself like a sort of mid- or late-Victorian person, not in outlook but in the position of writing a bit of poetry (we forget that George Eliot also wrote verse), writing novels, being interested in questions of the day and occasionally writing about them, and being interested in the work of other writers and occasionally writing about that. I'm not exactly an entertainer pure and simple, not exactly an artist pure and simple, certainly not an incisive critic of society, and certainly not a political figure, though I'm interested in politics. I think I'm just a combination of some of those things.

II
John Braine:
The Man at the Top

John Braine was born in Bradford in 1922 and was educated at St. Bede's Grammar School. After a variety of jobs he became, in 1940, an assistant at Bingley Public Library, where he worked (apart from a year in the Royal Navy) for the next eleven years. He became a full-time writer in 1957 and in 1966 left Yorkshire for Woking, where he now lives with his wife, son, and three daughters.

Since 1957, when *Room at the Top* was the bestseller, Braine has been an international name. His novel was translated into many languages and made into a film starring Laurence Harvey and Simone Signoret. He has written twelve books since—two of them thrillers, one a guide to novel writing, and a biography of J. B. Priestley. He is also a successful film critic, book reviewer, and television writer. When we met he was completing his new novel, *One and Last Love*. After a number of false starts, the writing was progressing satisfactorily. "It rather frightens me, in fact," he added in a voice swelled with a thick Yorkshire accent; "I'm learning things about myself which I didn't know before!" During the next days he kindly and patiently put at my disposal his time, experience, and hospitality. We talked for 26 hours—rather, he talked and I listened.

Braine does all of his writing in a tiny room on the top floor of a business building in Woking. The office contains his life: on the shelves are his manuscripts, notebooks, and rolls of galley proofs. There, too, are the books which since a child he has read for pleasure, including O'Hara

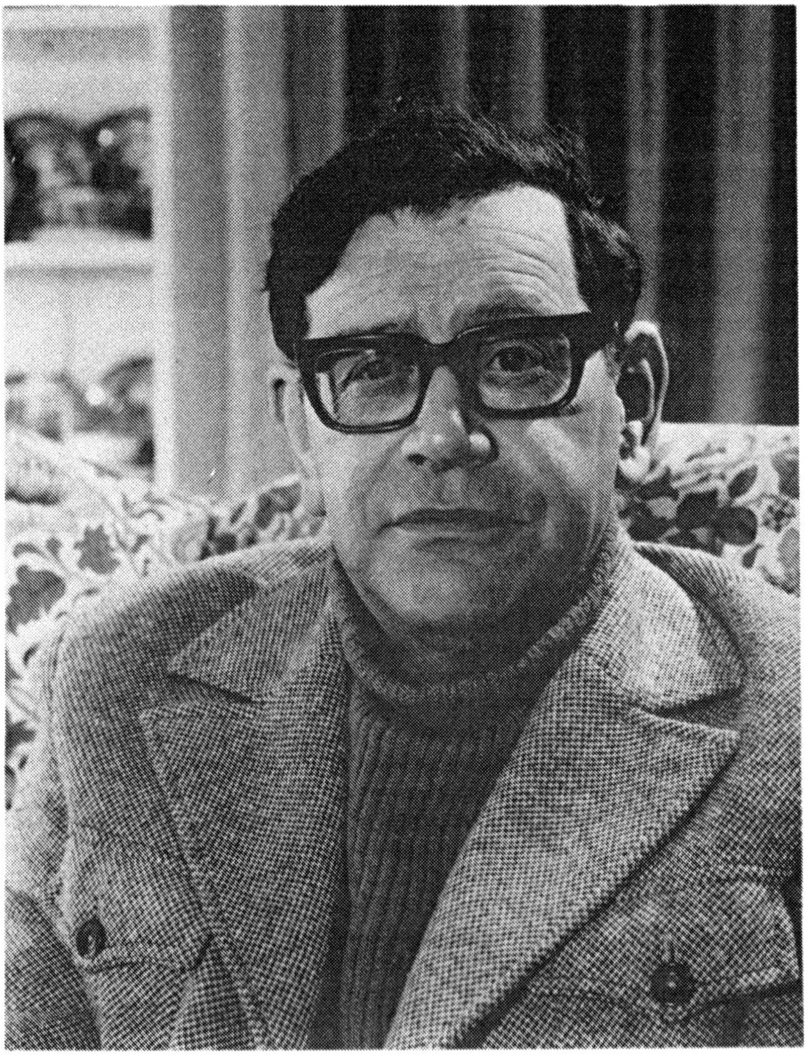

("An underrated writer"), Rilke ("I could quote reams of Rilke"), Fitzgerald, and, of course, Priestley. Braine looked younger than his 59 years. He is a large man, with a broad, not very straight back, and bowed shoulders. His approach to anyone new is one of open curiosity and friendliness. There was something about his pale blue eyes, as they looked from behind blackrimmed glasses, that suggested he takes in everything he sees. He is most concerned with getting to the facts, to the reality behind events and people. Despite the frustrations and disappointments which are the bitter but inevitable lot of his calling, Braine is not unhappy in his writing. As he once wrote of Priestley, he "know[s] what it's like down there in the blood and sand." He is an honest craftsman, skillful, successful in what he undertakes, and ready to persist against great odds.

We also visited his "home away from home"—Fleet Street—and walked from pub to pub to meet literary figures, editors, and a host of characters right out of the pages of Dickens. Lunch with Nicholas Bagnoll, literary reviewer for *The Daily Telegraph*, climaxed two very busy days.

JOHN BRAINE

DS: John Wain in his autobiography tells about seeing Kingsley Amis write a novel and enjoying it so much that he sat down himself and wrote *Hurry on Down*. Is there anything remotely like this in your experience? What suddenly made you want to write your first novel?

JB: Well, back in 1951—up until then I had a safe job at a public library—I left Yorkshire to become a freelance writer in London. I think now I must have been mad. Up until then I thought of myself as a poet and also as a social observer. I was a great admirer of Mayhew, and I thought it was quite enough just to look at things properly, not becoming concerned with what should be but always with what is. And I thought you start from there. That is, after all, how Dickens started. Everybody forgets that. Everybody thinks of the Pickwick Papers as being his first book. Well, that's not where he started. He started from observations. When I say observations, that means an awful lot of things. When I say seeing, that means all sorts of other things conveyed along with the seeing. I also thought of myself as a playwright. I was involved with amateur acting at the Bingley Little Theatre, in Yorkshire. I was a founder member there. I wasn't interested in amateur acting because I had any ambition to be an actor. I couldn't have been an actor.

I didn't want to be an actor. But the only way to learn how to write plays is to get practical experience on the stage. And I wrote a verse play, "The Desert in the Mirror," from Auden's quote which you'll probably recognize. I had it put on at the Bingley Little Theatre, not *by* the Little Theatre, but *at* the Little Theatre. The producer was a man called Donald Howarth. The play was a flop, but by then I was also writing articles for the newspapers. David Hammer, head of David Hammer Associates, my agent now, read a piece I had written about my Irish grandmother. He was very impressed with it. Paul Scott, who then worked for Highams (David Higham was an agent of the Harold Ober school and was agent for Dylan Thomas), asked me if I would like to be a client of theirs. I had a talk with Paul at his office, and he said he thought I had the makings of a novelist. I didn't really before then think of writing a novel, but I went away and started writing a novel. Then the Turnstile Press came to me with a proposition. Aylmer Vallance—an associated editor, I think—met me and we had a long talk. I told him I was thinking of writing a novel. He said that if I sent them a specimen chapter and a synopsis they'd subsidize me—if they liked it.

Well, I started work. But then I fell ill. And my mother died. And I had to go back to Yorkshire—that would be about December—but I wrote the specimen chapter and the synopsis. I sent it to Turnstile Press just before I went into the hospital in January, 1952. I really was ill. I had lost my voice and hadn't any money. Then the Turnstile Press rejected the chapter and synopsis. I didn't feel very happy. I was ill, I hadn't any money, I hadn't got a job, and the only thing I really could do when I went into the hospital was to begin the novel again. And that was *Room at the Top*. I just had to start from scratch.

DS: From your early experiences, what would you say is the most important thing about being a writer?

JB: J. B. Priestley said, as far as he was concerned, the most important thing about being a writer is not talent but character. It doesn't make any difference how brilliant you are if you don't actually do the work. I met lots of people when I was young who were far more clever than me. But I'm still writing, and they aren't. And I've known lots of instances like that. I look back to 1957, when there were lots of bright people, bright writers around, who wrote one novel, and then seemed to have disappeared. They aren't around any longer. Well, obviously what Priestley says is an overstatement. But the novel is a longterm project always. Even the shortest novel is a longterm project. It isn't writing a review, or even quite a long article or story. I haven't written many short stories. I do enjoy writing them, but there never is the time. I never wrote many short stories before *Room at the Top* because there was no market.

DS: What is the essential difference between writing a short story and writing a novel?

JB: With a short story, you can see the end of it. You can carry the whole idea in your head and that's very exciting. I just write out a very brief synopsis and I go ahead and can finish a 3500-word short story in about a week. And then it's published as I wrote it. But with a novel you've got to carry so much in your head. I'm working on a novel now— *One and Last Love*. It must be finished by October. I do have a very brief synopsis, with things in it like characters' ages, names. I give you my word that, although I know all these things, I keep on having to check. I discovered looking at the first chapter that I put the hero's age down on one page as 54, whereas he's 56. And I've got a reasonably good memory. It can miss a cylinder. It can misfire now and again, but sooner or later it does work. Indeed, my memory is like the Model T. It's very primitive, and ugly. Maybe now and again it gives up the ghost. It stops for a while. It wheezes and sputters, but then one gives it a sharp kick in the right place and it sputters on. It keeps on working. But even then one can find oneself forgetting things in a novel. Also, whenever one starts a novel, one can find oneself thinking, "How will I ever finish it? All those thousands and thousands of words." You've got to keep the shape of it in your head. You've got to be sure of the shape of it. And I always write the end first. Otherwise I don't know where I'm heading. It's a very difficult job indeed.

DS: Do you agree with John Fowles, who is on record as having said that a novelist is born, not made?

JB: Quite honestly, I think you're born a novelist or you're not. It's nothing to do with literary ability or intelligence. You can be a very good writer, but not be a novelist. Everybody thinks he can write a novel. I don't know why it is, but they honestly do. And they can't, you know. Generally speaking, you can find this to be true with academics. Universities are full of people who know all about the novel, and all about writing it, and they all think they can write novels, and some of them do write a novel, one novel, and then they discover their mistake. It's nothing to do with intelligence at all. It's just having this narrative ability, that's all that matters. But you have it or you haven't it.

So it is genetic, in the same way that being a general is genetic. Napoleon, Wellington were great generals because they were born great generals. They weren't bred to be so. It comes out of a fundamental question of character. At one time most educators, psychologists believed in economic determinism. But more and more they have come around to the belief in about 80% heredity with regards to character, intelligence, and so forth. A lousy environment can of course wreck this. If it's a marvelous environment, it can bring out the utmost of an average person. So I agree with Fowles.

DS: What effect did your mother have on you?

JB: My mother had a strong personality. She died in a road accident in 1951. She was a librarian and got the job before the war simply by pestering the local councilor. At that time the Irish weren't that popular in Bradford. Generally speaking, the Irish would only get laboring jobs, unskilled jobs. The general feeling about the Irish was that they were boozy, violent, uncouth, and Catholic, too. Yes, there was discrimination. And so it was unheard of for an Irish Catholic to get a job as a librarian. But she got it by sheer perseverance. And she passed this strength on to me.

I was the first-born. In Cyril Connolly's book, *Enemies of Promise*, he talks about the headmaster's wife in a small prep school. She was a very good teacher with a very strong personality. She pushed all those boys. Connolly said about her: "She supercharged us like little Alfa-Romeos for the Brooklands of life." That's what my mother did for me. She supercharged me. From the first time I could remember, looking right back, I knew that she would assure me I was handsome, irresistibly charming, and a genius. And she expected great things of me. And I'd do great things. As one grows older one looks in the mirror and realizes: no, I'm not handsome, not irresistibly charming, and not a genius. I was intelligent enought to realize this couldn't be true. But deep down, because my mother had implanted that idea, I believe it to this day. I got used to being pushed.

DS: Are your memories of primary school good ones?

JB: I had a sound education in primary school from five to eleven. I was the teacher's pet. Good at English. I used to bring flowers to teachers. I was really a little apple polisher. I was very happy in primary school. Women teachers then were spinsters. Their potential husbands had been killed in the 1914 war. They were dedicated, as in *The Corn is Green*. I was doubly privileged. I always felt I would have been better if I had had women teachers at grammar school.

DS: You relate well to women?

JB: I prefer to work with women, as a matter of fact. In the library, you tend to get more women in senior positions than in other branches of local government. I don't know why, but it is so. As librarian, I was used to having women in senior positions. I could get around them easier. Don't get me wrong. I'm not talking about sex here. My manhood wasn't threatened.

I was born essentially to be a victim of women. You have to pay for everything in this life. If you're mom's favorite, you will pay for it. You won't be henpecked, but you'll be especially vulnerable to women. Once women know that you're on their side, they'll somehow or other carry you along. Without sweating about it you'll be able to understand women. The price you pay is that you'll always be vulnerable to women and to some extent a victim of women.

DS: Getting back to the thought that a novelist is born, are there any exceptions to this "rule"?

JB: Lots of other things are terribly important, but the only exception I know to this rule is Lionel Trilling's *The Middle of the Journey*. This is one of my favorite books. It's always been a key book for me since I first discovered it. It's a marvelous novel, but it makes me angry. I really get vexed about it. Because when I first came to it, I had only known Trilling as a brilliant critic, an interpreter—not an analyzer, an interpreter. I respect that. I don't see writing as being graded, with the creative man at the top, then the underlings. A true critic—someone like Trilling—is as much a writer as a novelist is. Before I opened Trilling's novel, I was hoping it would be a mess—very clever, but dead. I really did feel that anybody who was so good a critic couldn't also be a good novelist. He'd have no right to be. It wasn't his job. With his other books I'd always thought: "This is brilliant, this is marvelous, this is really good—and then, oh my God, I couldn't really do this." Then I'd think to myself, rather smugly, "Well, all right, Mr. Trilling, so I can't do what you do, but then you can't do what I do." But then you discover in *The Middle of the Journey* that indeed he can. Mind you, he only did it once. He didn't try to repeat it. But this is a superb novel. He breaks many of the rules. But then why should we have all these rules?

DS: What advice would you give to a young writer today?

JB: If you want to be a writer, you must have in the end a clear, cool, sensible mind. Someone with common sense. Somebody who will do his duty, who has got to be in charge. Also, you shouldn't write about other writers. You shouldn't write about intellectuals, academics. To a certain extent this is true. My advice to people who want to write novels is, don't write about writers. Because on a whole their jobs are not really interesting to the average reader. They don't involve enough action. They're too much in the ivory tower. But then as I've grown older and I think of *The Middle of the Journey*, and I also think of Alison Lurie (whom I absolutely love), I say why not?

The advice I gave to the people in my novel class at Purdue University was, for God's sake, keep away from artists. If you write a novel about an artist or a writer, you run out of material pretty quickly. One writes a novel about a writer who is writing a novel about a writer—and so it goes on.

DS: I understand you're writing a novel about a novelist now.

JB: Yes. *One and Last Love* is not about other people but about myself. That sounds pretty boring. I promise you that it won't be. Anyway, at a certain stage in one's career one can do what one likes. One's earned the right. All that matters is, does it work? An example: my novel is about a middle-aged writer who for the first time in his life has a happy love affair. This goes on for a long time and it actually pleases him. And he says in the first chapter, of course, this novel is not autobiographical, mainly because that would bore you. You don't want to hear about me. This novel isn't autobiographical, it's biographical. It's about you. But I'm not trying to tell you how you should live, because you must never listen to anybody who tells you how you should live. What it really means is they want you to dance to their tune and sing their song. That's absolutely wrong. Make your own dance, your own music. Again he says in the novel, quoting Cocteau, "The muse ushers the artist into an empty room, and points silently at the tightrope." My hero says that up until recently, this is essentially what I've been doing. And I've been very good on the tightrope, and of course I have an audience. But I'm not doing it for an audience, I'm doing it for myself. Whatever I do on the tightrope, I do for myself. But now I'm going to come down, forget about the tightrope. I'm going to come down and I'm going to walk among the audience. I'm going to speak directly to the audience, and I'm going to talk to them about themselves. But how do you explain this? I refuse to. The explanation is the novel. Because words mean what they mean. They can't be explained.

DS: You mentioned to me that one critic actually anticipated this novel in a review he had written of *Waiting for Sheila*.

JB: Yes. In 1976, in a very good review of *Waiting for Sheila*, Ferdinand Mount says that someday, hopefully, Braine will write a book "700 pages, rampantly self-indulgent, violently inconsequential—and irresistible." The curious thing is, I didn't come across this review until after I'd started *One and Last Love*. And I realized that this was an exact description of what I wanted to do. In fact, when I get the time I must write to Ferdinand Mount and tell him how extraordinary his comment was. How in the hell did you know?

DS: Was it difficult to get started with the writing of *One and Last Love*?

JB: At first I had in mind a family saga, and I tried and tried for eighteen months to write it, but got nowhere. Other things intervened, including writing a three-part television adaptation. Then in December I thought it through and became more and more worried. I realized I had to start again. So I began the first draft and finished it in April of this year (1980)—60,000 words. Then I began the second draft in May and I will finish in October. I know I will finish because the first draft is good. It works.

I am putting absolutely everything in it. It occurs within a four year period, going backwards from time to time, but only when relevant. It will probably spill over into two more books at least. All sorts of memories can come into it which one does transform into something totally different. One must be careful to always keep in mind what's the central story, and the digressions may appear to be casual, but they have all got to be relevant. It is in fact sort of a Will Rogers' act. You remember: he began with a lariat, did tricks with it, and the talk was something to occupy the ears of the audience. In time the audience stops thinking about the lariat. His monologues appeared terribly casual—in the Huck Finn tradition here—but it was too damn casual not to be highly organized. He was an artist of the order of Bing Crosby. Too, too damn casual. There must be a great deal of emotional force behind that performance. Otherwise, it would be dead, neutral without life. Behind his performance he must be a highly neurotic, a highly emotional man. But then all that matters about any artist is his work.

DS: Was *Waiting for Sheila* an experiment in a sense?

JB: Well, experiment is the wrong word. The thing about *Waiting for Sheila*, which I'm very fond of, is that I was trying something new. It observes the unities, actually. It doesn't leave Jim's home. It takes place within a few hours. I actually adapted it for television. It worked very well, although a one-shot play is really too little space and it needed about three parts at least, each one hour long.

But the experiment there was keeping the unities, and also looking at an aspect of sex that most people never look at. The strange thing is that whenever anybody thinks about sex, they think in an almost primitive way. They think that you're either one thing or the other. And a chap is either impotent or he's potent. That's it. There's nothing in between. Oh, perhaps he's potent most of the time and then he has too many drinks and he's terribly depressed. Or he meets a real ballbreaker, which has the same effect. But no, it's much more various. One has actually come across people who have had this problem. What I was surprised to find out about *Waiting for Sheila* was this: you may be talking with somebody about it, somebody may be interviewing you about it on radio, and they go on about Jim not being terribly good sexually. Then I realized that he hadn't absolutely read the book! Jim is virile. He's very good with Sheila. There's nothing wrong with him. In one way Jim says, why should I worry? I am a man. This is what the whole book is about—what being a man is. Being a man is not simply being a performer. Sex isn't about performance. It's much more complicated than that. Manhood isn't being macho, about being the chap who can beat any man in the bar and can fuck any woman. Actually, when a chap starts saying things like that he's headed for trouble. For terrible trouble. Particularly with sex. I think that was the trouble with old Hemingway in the end. You know, he was thinking wrongly about sex. Mixing it up with war.

DS: Sexuality is a central interest of yours in *Stay With Me Till Morning*.

JB: In that novel I ask, what are the facts about sex? Hard to answer. Kinsey, for example, asked a certain number of men this question, but who is answering? The sort of man who answers a survey about sex. They do not tell you what *everybody* does sexually. So I just listen, eavesdrop virtually. I have discovered one general principle regarding sex: whenever anybody tells you they haven't, they have. Whenever anybody says they have, they haven't. This is true for most human behavior. We don't really know. The most we can say is well, in some fields of human behavior it's recorded.

DS: As a writer then, your primary concern is with what the facts are?

JB: As an artist, I've got to be writing about life as it is. If the world's going to survive, then let's get rid of the intellectuals and the theorizers. Let's not have any theories. Let's start finding out what the truth is. And this is damned difficult. All I can say is that when I was younger everything was much easier to work out. In one way more people seem to have power. And in another way, fewer. There is a great distance between us and those in charge. But if you ask who has got the power, no one will tell you. They keep fobbing you off. I read a very good article in *Encounter* a long time ago, about the international bureaucracy. And the great point it made was this: that the bureaucrat in the United States, in Russia, and in Europe are all on the same side. They have an identity and a common purpose which has nothing to do with the people on whose behalf they are supposed to operate. If you get an American bureaucrat and a Russian bureaucrat together with an European bureaucrat—they're all the same sort of person. And they're absolutely different from the mass of people. Their aims are different. I don't have the time to work all this out. I have to depend upon other people. I would want people of your age to start thinking about this. Step-by-step. Don't come to any hasty conclusions. Just decide what the hell you can do about it.

DS: How did you feel about being identified with the so-called "Angry Young Men?"

JB: Well, in the first instance it's better to be identified publicly than not to be identified at all. And this is relevant. This is a question which you are bound to ask. It's like when people say, "Oh, surely, mustn't it be awful to be known as the author of just one book?" And I say, "Well, it's better to be known as the author of one book than not to be known at all." If ever you get a certain kind of journalist who says what actually isn't true, "Well, don't you think you're a has-been?" I always quote something that Reggie Kray—the gangster—said when he was being led away from the dock after the guilty verdict and somebody yelled out, "Reggie, what's it feel like to be a has-been?" He said, "It's better to be a has-been than a never-was." No, I wasn't bothered about that at the time. The fact is, the whole Angry Young Men business is nonsense. It's entirely nonsense because in England there haven't been for a long time any real literary groups. This is not an idea that appeals to English writers. It does appeal quite seriously to continental writers. One has listened to a Robbe-Grillet and Marguerite Durras on the same platform together—all very boring because their books are boring. Nevertheless, one respected them. It's just a question of the continental writer thinking that it is quite natural and right that writers get together and work out a common program.

But British writers just aren't like that. They just don't work that way. There never was a group, and all the people who have been labeled Angry Young Men are all very different. In fact, England being a small country, I know most of them. We used to meet every week at Bertorellis in Soho. Anthony Burgess, Bernard Levin, Bob Conquest used to come as well. All sorts of people. Tony Powell used to come. We were a loosely organized group around 1966. There wasn't any formal organization, any committee, meetings, anything like that. But we haven't been together for several years. I think that life has been getting rougher and rougher, and people can't afford the time anymore.

DS: But didn't you share common political ideals?

JB: The only thing we had in common was that we weren't left-wing. We just refused to accept the liberal package deal. Around 1967 we sent a letter to the *Times*. Ten or fifteen of us signed it and supported the American position in Vietnam. We didn't say we approved of everything; indeed, we didn't. Although Vietnam is a hell of a long way from us, if they take over Vietnam, they're that much nearer, and that can't be good for us. Very simple reasoning. All hell popped. There were indignant letters to the *Times*. We got lots of absolutely lunatic letters. A group of academics took out a full page ad in the *Times* condemning us. We did give the group a name after that. We called it the Fascist Beast Luncheon Group.

DS: Do you see it as ironic that some of the so-called Angry Young Men—such as yourself, Wain, Amis, Cooper, and others—were writing in a traditional style?

JB: Well, there hasn't really been all that much experimentation in England for a while. Perhaps a novel is different from the visual arts in this. But when I look at what happened in the visual arts, I think it is a good thing on the whole, because the visual arts by and large become more and more alienated from the public. This is also true for drama to some extent. There seems to be some fundamental breakdown. But as soon as you start saying this, someone will say, "Oh, I suppose you just want the well-made play." No indeed, you don't. You are being specific and saying that with the British novel you don't have much choice. If you are going to survive as a novelist, you can't experiment. One doesn't want to experiment. I'm very interested in technique, and I am always trying something new. But experiments one has seen in the novel seem to me not to work at all. I don't think there's any serious artistic purpose behind them. Whenever I see that a novel is experimental, I know that it's the work of an incompetent. Somebody just thinks up an idea with the front half of his brain. He's not really thinking deeply. He hopes merely that it will excite notice. He doesn't have any serious artistic purpose. If you're going to write a novel, you must be understandable. Not that I worry. If I understand myself that's quite enough. That's all I worry about. I don't worry about people not picking up allusions, because how can you tell which allusions people will pick up? You have got to please yourself.

DS: To whom is your first duty as a writer? To yourself? Or to the reader?

JB: Your first duty is to yourself, because you're the only person you really know anything about. If a writer himself understands what he is writing, if he really knows what he is writing about, if he knows what his words mean, then his audience will know. As long as he's writing sincerely, as long as he's doing the best job he can, he doesn't have to worry about explaining things and writing down, ever. They will pick it up. It's rather like the business of *Room at the Top*. The hero and a lot of characters speak with a Yorkshire accent. The experts said: "They aren't going to understand that in America. It's going to be dead in America." But at that time lots of people from the film industry had this idea—they still have—that you should do films for an international market with an international accent, not particularly English, not particularly American, so that they can understand it in both countries. The result is an accent which is neither one damn thing nor another. And it has no flavor. But nobody anywhere had any difficulty. If you write well enough and know what you mean, then people will pick it up somehow or other. They understand from the context. They don't work it out intellectually. One has this experience very often if working in television. You're watching the rushes. You'll say a certain shot is right. You know it's right, but you can't analyze it. Possibly you could analyze it if you took a long time out. Even then you might be wrong. Why do certain words work and why do not certain words? Most of the time when I am writing I play it by ear.

DS: Do you have an audience in mind when you write?

JB: A writer is not like an actor. An actor has got to have an audience before he can work. He doesn't exist without an audience. We as writers are doing our jobs by ourselves, but even then you need an audience. And when you look at the great Victorians, particularly when you look at Dickens—he is not the sort of man who would lick anybody's boot. He was an independent man. A creator. But when he wrote, one feels it's going out to the readers. You feel that current. He wasn't working out formulas to please them. He was just interested in reaching out to them. I'm not here to talk to myself, after all. I want to talk *to* somebody. And get a response. I need that. And so did Dickens and other 19th century writers. The current was there up to about 1939.

But somehow or other, in recent years, it's been lost. It's gone. I don't know how it's gone, but it's gone. Not in myself. I've always felt it. But generally speaking, that's one of the troubles with all the arts today. I've always hung onto this feeling that I'm in touch with my readers. I feel it more and more. And in *One and Last Love* I'm indulging in it and feeling very happy. It is not a question of my working out formulas which will please them. It is a question simply of needing this relationship with my audience. But I feel generally, as far as a novelist is concerned—indeed, as far as all of the arts are concerned—that something has gone. The current very largely is not there.

DS: Is the same true for television?

JB: In the average successful American television show, there's this feeling of alienation. The people who wrote the script and put the whole damn thing together did it cynically. They're a small elite. They are very adept, but they use formulas. With certain British shows—for example, *Coronation Street*—with all its faults, one knows that the people who produce and write it are really wanting to reach out to the audience. They know what the audience feels.

DS: What about American writers?

JB: As Cyril Connolly said a long time ago about American writers, the average American novelist can be guilty of a fearful doggishness, a false mateyness. But the impression one gets from say O'Hara is that of a man saying to you: "Listen. I think they're going to be interested in all this. Look what happened to me!" O'Hara was in touch with his audience. But there again, if you try to explain this to people, they make all sorts of false assumptions. They assume that in the first instance you only care about making money. Well, you've got to care about making money because you've got to pay the bills like everybody else. And then they assume that you're not an artist. Well, yes I am an artist. But in all the arts the intellectual has taken over. The theorizers have taken over—that's to say, people who think in the abstract. A certain kind of academic writes books about this writer and that writer. And they're grading all the damn time, using rigid standards. One has got to conform to these standards. And you listen to them talk sometimes and give you a lecture, and you think when they've finished talking about a poem or a novel—where has the pleasure principle gone? He's only talking about this poem or this novel because it's still giving people a lot of pleasure. But the Common Reader's disregarded. The thing is, if you really want to be a true interpreter, then you've never got to cease to be the Common Reader. As Virginia Woolf said very wisely, the Common Reader is the final judge. The only reason *Moby Dick* has survived and there's a flourishing Melville industry—not that he flourished when he was alive, poor devil!—is not because of the efforts of the academics, but because people continue to enjoy reading it.

DS: What then to you is an ideal reader?

JB: Well, if I did have an ideal reader it would be somebody who was reasonably literate, who has done a certain amount of reading. It doesn't necessarily have to be an academic. But somebody who does read, principally for enjoyment, and doesn't actually have any sort of theories or any sort of snobbishness. The strange thing about literature, about the novel, is this: all sorts of unlikely people can produce great art, can produce a great novel. Really, being able to write well is rather like the way in which grace can visit people. I'm not terribly religious, but one knows something about it and how it works. And many critics are always thinking in terms of what should be and what shouldn't be. They think, "Well, if you're going to be saved you must abide by certain rules." I have a feeling that very often some of the reviewers look at people like me and they say, "Well, it's not fair. Why him? I could have handled all this much better."

DS: Do you read your critics?

JB: I used to receive clippings from a clippings agency. About four years ago I stopped bothering. I discovered if they were nasty, they were depressing—even though you think the person who has written it is an absolute idiot, which most of them are. If somebody spat in your face, although obviously he'd be a slob, you wouldn't like it, would you? I knew that if they were good, I'd see them anyway. A lot of the reviews of my second novel, *The Vodi*, were very nasty indeed. If I had written a book like *Room at the Top*, they would have said, "Oh well, the same again. Hasn't he got any invention? Has he run out of inspiration? He's a flash in the pan." Well, I wrote a book which is about an entirely different sort of man. They said, "Oh well, that was easy. He's just done the opposite!" You can't win, you see.

The strange thing about *The Vodi* is this: it had some good reviews, some nice reviews, but when we brought out the paperback it came to nothing. And then Penguin just let it go out of print. But in hardback—and that's the test of a novel, that's what counts—it reprinted and it kept on reprinting. And all big prints. And it kept on selling steadily. Last year, I revised it. Not major revisions, but it was a question of clearing up several errors which had crept in. There was just a little clarification, but no basic alterations. Then it was reprinted in hardback in the revised edition.

DS: Many writers speak of the mysterious process involved in the creation of a character. Could you relate this to the creation of Xavier Flynn, your hero in both *The Pious Agent* and *Fingers of Fire*?

JB: Oh, much of Xavier is me, although God knows I've never been in the secret service and wouldn't be much good at it at all. I'm not a violent man. I'm cautious. I want to die on my bed of old age. But Xavier is also based on other people. I start off with a character I know personally. Sometimes someone one doesn't know personally has been seen about, or met briefly. This is over-simplifying, but I take a bit from one, a bit from another, and another bit, and then take a story, something that has happened to somebody else, and mix it all together. It's a bit like this—a terribly obvious illustration—where you get a man and woman and they go to bed together, and nine months later you've got an entirely different human being. There may be likenesses, but he or she, the new human being, is totally different.

It is a mysterious process. Before I created Xavier I saw a newspaper story which said the Department of Defense has a private chapel, and it's not financed by public money. It's for people to be quiet in. It isn't Catholic or Protestant. I suddenly realized something: can't a secret agent be a Catholic? There must be some Catholic secret agents. There are Catholic soldiers. One thinks about giving the reader shocks. That's the basis of all fiction. You can give them different kinds of shock, but you must always keep on giving them. You had great shock values there. Even then the reviewers never got it straight. They'd say in their reviews: whenever Xavier kills somebody in the line of duty he says an act of contrition. No, I didn't say that. When Xavier kills somebody in the line of duty he doesn't have to say an act of contrition. He hasn't committed a sin. He prays for his enemy's soul. No, he said an act of contrition after he poked a woman. In case he died afterwards and he went to hell, which he would if not in the state of grace. And then they all started getting shocked about that and said this shouldn't be. I would say, well, it isn't my job to judge. That is how Xavier *is*.

I liked him myself, and I was sympathetic with him. He's a nice human being. He's a decent chap. At one moment there's a police officer who gets rid of the bodies afterwards and says what a nasty, dirty job it is. Xavier says, "Oh, I'm one of the nasty ones. No one would want to go near me because I'm one of the nasty ones, but where would anybody be without us?" That's something I think about quite frequently more and more. Somebody has got to do certain things. This haunts me more and more. It is one of the things I was trying to say in both books. It's all right being high-minded, and nice and civilized, and reasonable, but who'll do the dirty work? And would *I* do it?

DS: Could you say something about your working methods, your routine for a day?

JB: Yes, it's quite simple. I come into my office around 9:30 in the morning. I brew myself a cup of strong tea, and I read the *Guardian*. I hate the paper. It's a lousy newspaper, and thoroughly English liberal, which is worse than United States liberal. Mind you, there's some good articles in there, very well-written. I would say it's the best magazine in Fleet Street. There's always something in it to start the adrenalin going—it's so damned stupid, but clever with it. And then about 10:30 I put down something in my diary. It's not terribly intimate. I just put down whatever occurs to me—a sort of loosening up. Then I begin to work, and I keep on about to 12:45. And then, although it's not precisely the same every day, I walk over to the library and get amongst other people. The important thing is this: one is amongst other people, but one isn't involved. So I've got somewhere to sit down where I can write and think. And thinking gets more and more difficult for me. I'm not terribly clever, but I'm thorough. I want to get things right. What does somebody look like? Sound like? What do they say? The wonderful thing is this: once you know about reality, revelation starts, intensity starts. So I walk along to the library. All that I really want is something readable. Something to read while I eat. It might be a novel. It might not be a novel. And then I come along back to my office, I eat my lunch, drink a mug of tea, and I read the book to relax. Then when I've finished eating I have half an hour's rest. No matter how busy I am I let go and don't worry. If I'm working very hard I don't bother, but most days I have it. And then I work from 2:30 to 6:00, and I go home three nights out of five. I eat what everybody else is eating, and that's my main meal of the day. I read, or watch television, just relax, and about 10:00 I go to bed. I read about an hour or so, have a cup of tea, a very small snack, and I go to sleep as if hit over the head. so it goes on. Friday I go to London.

DS: Do you keep a notebook?

JB: No, I keep a diary. Some volumes of my diary are at the Bradford Public Library, others here in my office. The current volume here, I've nearly filled up. But I don't write my diaries for publication. Just for loosening up. Sometimes I think I ought to be like the real writers—

the continentals are better at this than we are, actually. You take somebody really good like Thomas Mann or Rilke—I love Rilke; I could quote reams of Rilke—who worked at being artists. They made a great production of it. An artist lives in a certain way and sits at his desk and produces great thoughts. The trouble with me is I don't think in terms of great thoughts. I think in terms of reality. On the other hand, I would not want to be the traditional drunken poet. It is all right now and again. In fact, it is very nice and can help you to relax. It takes the pressure off. It's all right being self-indulgent from time to time, but not as a permanent thing. As a matter of fact, no matter what people may say, what is essential in my life is to deliver so many words. I'm a great counter of words. And I know as long as I produce the words, deliver the words, even if those words are not right, I'm okay.

DS: You have been invited to American universities. What do you think of the growing habit of English writers associating themselves with universities, not merely in the U.S., but here as well?

JB: Well, I was invited to be a writer-in-residence once. I've had tentative dealings with other American universities. I would like to go again, I don't think for too long. I would like to organize it better beforehand than I did the last time. But actually, as far as English universities are concerned, it is a question of economics. As far as I know—I don't know an awful lot about it—the sort of jobs they offer at English universities really aren't worthwhile. I once looked into—I wasn't actually invited—what they offered to the writer-in-residence at the University of East Anglia. As far as I could see, what one was offered was 1000 pounds for a term of four months. You get a furnished flat, reasonably large, thrown in. I didn't see anything about free travel, and what would be expected of one in return for that. The money is quite honestly not going to take you very far. Put all other considerations aside and consider the fact that if you're a writer you need a bit of travel, you need to meet people. It's not a question of living high. In addition to everything else you'd be expected to do a certain amount of teaching of creative writing and run cultural activities. Organize a literary festival. Arrange for speeches. All the rest of it. That takes time.

At Purdue University I discovered about teaching. I'll tell this much about teaching—and I'm not telling it just to please you. Before I taught for the first time in my life, I used to think that teachers shouldn't be paid, they should pay us to teach. The first morning of teaching I did lasted two fifty-minute periods. In the interval I just went to the lounge and had cup after cup of coffee. I felt so tired. I can never remember being so tired. I went onto the sofa and I slept for five hours. I have worked six hours writing, particularly in television, and I've been tired when I finished. But it's a different sort of tiredness—a physical tiredness, it's healthy. But teaching: you're *giving out*.

DS: What in your opinion is the situation of the writer in America?

JB: For the last four or five years, it's been the era of the blockbuster and formula fiction. Once upon a time the average American publisher believed in the backlist principle and supported the steady sellers. And they'd take risks. By and large as long as a novel had some literary merit, they would publish it. They wanted to make a profit, of course. Most of them did. But more and more now it's been taken over by the sales department and the result is this: you're getting deals now in the region of five million dollars. And people who could get published before just can't get published any more. They're not interested in the smaller seller, even the steady seller. Well, in the end I have a shrewd feeling that they'll get their fingers burned. The trouble with this idea of blockbusters is that you stand to make a big profit, but you also stand to make a big loss. There are no sure things. I cling to this, and it doesn't make any difference what the experts tell me. I know it's true.

DS: What about the sale of your own novels in America?

JB: You know, everything's going wrong. I realized that when I got to Purdue in 1978. I had been complaining about this to my American agent and getting nowhere. Then I got to Purdue and discovered that everybody knew my work, but I discovered there were none of my books in stock. I complained about this but got no further. Then a friend of mine from England told me about Methuen, Inc., being set up in New York. They are an offshoot of Associated Book Publishers, the parent company of my British publisher, Eyre Methuen. I set it up, and the result is that now Methuen, Inc. has published *Room at the Top*, *Life at the Top*, and *Waiting for Sheila*. And that's the odd thing. They've been going only about two years. Quite obviously these are early days, and one doesn't know what will happen in the future. But they've got to set up a sales organization. It isn't so much a question of doing things in a big way and having high power people doing a campaign. It's something very simple and fundamental: one has your publisher's representatives who get to know where all the bookshops are and get the booksellers to stock the books. And if he doesn't do that, then the publisher is sunk and so is the poor writer.

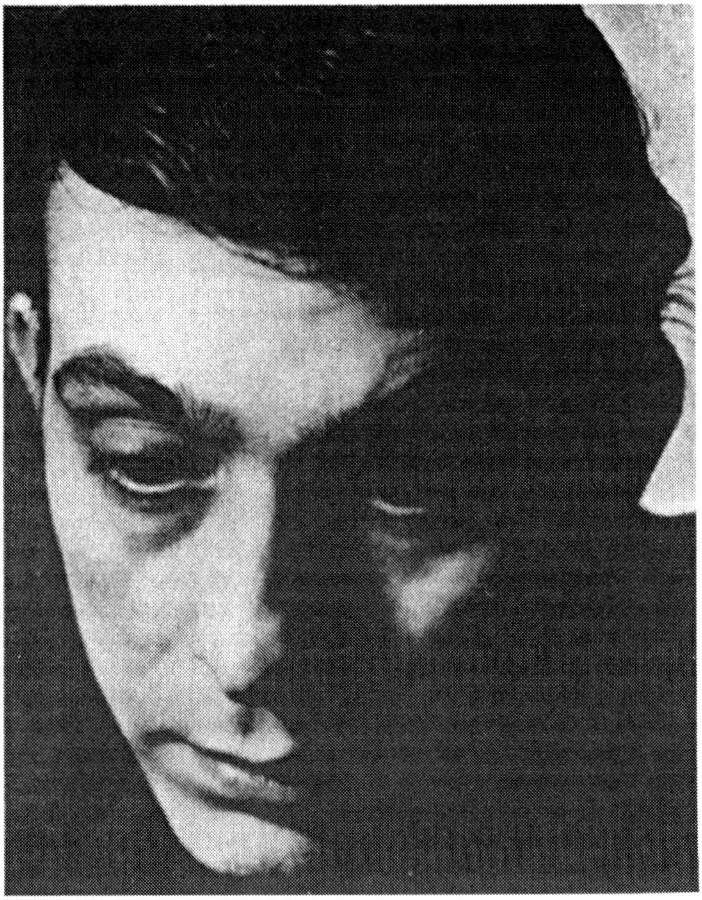

III
Bill Hopkins:
Looking for the Revolutionary

Bill Hopkins was born in 1918 in Cardiff, South Wales, and was educated privately. He worked in journalism and publishing from 1946 to 1957. His first and only novel, *The Divine and the Decay* (1958), came under strong critical attack in the British press. Associated with the Angry Young Men—especially with Colin Wilson—Hopkins faded from the literary scene in the early 1960s. The interview took place in Wilson's room at the Curzon Hotel, London.

BILL HOPKINS

DS: How did you feel when literary journalists in the 1950s and later identified you as a so-called Angry Young Man?

BH: With considerable foreboding. It was the equivalent of someone shouting "Stop, thief!" as one strolls down the road, and, of course, started off the pack in pursuit. The first use of the phrase "Angry Young Man" was purely for the sake of calling attention to a new sensation—an unheard-of thing, an English literary school. No such entity existed, of course. But then the phrase began to take on a sinister meaning: the Angry Young Men weren't an innocent group of writers and dreamers, but were enemies of Society. This gave license for stupid and uninformed attacks and eventually brainwashed the public into a murderous hostility that destroyed all hopes of effecting a change in public thinking. Of course, England was very sick at the time, and we were very young and hopeful. A place of sickness isn't the best place for youth, and really it was a case of the wrong place, the wrong people, the wrong time, and quite the wrong messages. New life is a terrible accusation against death, I think. Looking back, I see it all quite clearly as an assassination plot, a time when England decided thinking was too painful and certainly wasn't about to restart with us. Unlike the others—Colin Wilson, John Osborne and John Wain, who soldiered on grimly—I shrugged, packed my bags, and took off to another place.

DS: How different from today was the era of the 1950s?

BH: Well, really, Britain was dying then, and didn't know why. It also did not want anyone to mention it, on the old English principle that if something is passed over in silence, then eventually it goes away. Today, our old country knows it has terminal cancer and howls in agony, not caring if the whole world hears and shudders at the collapse. It's quite frightening in a sense, since pride and camouflage were such English things once. But at last we've reached the lip of the precipice, and one feels everywhere the gathering desperation of a national moment. Historically this time is more important by far than the Fifties, because now we are forming up in conscious ranks for the battle that will decide whether we can spring from the besiegement of national extinction in one form to a new form more aerial and indestructible in which the British can find another commencement to their destiny. All reason, fact, and history tell us that it is impossible and even, in an evolutionary sense, impermissible. But yet, knowing that, the battle lines are recruiting visibly and drums are beginning to throb from the center of cancer. It really is quite stirring and ennobling to take one's place again. The night is ending with all its fears, and now a new aristocracy is about to be born in struggle and no more from inheritance.

The difference in terms of time, to answer your question, is that the Fifties were not a time to put one's head above the barricade: today, the issues are clear and the atmosphere is cleaner. I mean that honesty and desperation have met and joined in their natural course. The view is quite different. For the first time in our life time, the unbelievable is not only possible but achievable. Of course, hope is a madness; but who walks on water without it?

DS: How do you see yourself as different from your contemporaries at that time?

BH: Because they have to write for money, basically, so they've written a lot of things that I think they'll regret. They've wasted a lot of their vitality. You know, I met Somerset Maugham towards the end of his life. During the course of the conversation I said: "Do you regret anything in your life?" He was about eighty then but still alert. He said: "Frankly, I regret virtually everything I've ever written. I'd stop its publication now." He meant that everything he had written seemed hopelessly trivial to what he was seeing with his last eyes of life. I see most of my contemporaries caught in the same fame-making syndrome, and clanking away with words which can only be summed up in the last analysis as trivial. Having to make one's living by writing and navigating everything to catch approval or even popularity mutilates more than it energizes, I think. I was always too ecstatic to contemplate clipping my wings for that role. Besides that, I know the marvelous things in life are only possible in privacy and silence. My contemporaries had other ideas, and possibly still have. But it must be very disillusioning for them when they meet the people who like their world. The real difference I see, apart from motivation and means (which are the outcome only of circumstances), is only in aim. Mine is perhaps too fanatic, demanding, and passionate. I don't regret it; and I certainly can't change it. Fortunately, I don't have to starve because it's so. In a sense, I feel that I'm cursed; but in another sense, blessed with more magic than one has a right to expect.

DS: Your first novel, *The Divine and the Decay*, was severely criticized, and your second novel, *Time and Totality*, got burnt in a fire when you had almost finished it. You must have been terribly discouraged.

BH: Not really. *The Divine and the Decay* was completely misunderstood, so the severe criticism was based invariably on the wrong grounds. When someone has deliberately written a novel that turns away from the form of other novels, how on earth can it be faulted because of its departure points? I found the conventional novel stupid, boring, and repetitive in every way. I had no intention of continuing it. The reviewers called the jump I made a jump to madness. But I notice that my novel is finding echoes everywhere nowadays. As for the novels they recommended, who wants them nowadays? These gentlemen are responsible for the novel form dying, and now the public have turned away in boredom to reading biographies and history instead. If I may say so, we'll have to make bigger jumps than *The Divine and the Decay*—to much further points of "madness"—before we recapture an audience to literature again. Certainly, explicit sex situations, banal sentimentality, or whining humanism aren't capable of the propulsion needed.

The burning of *Time and Totality* was probably the best thing that could have happened. It was the wrong time for it. I kept the excitement it gave me and directed it towards living with a ferocity and appetite that amounted to a rebirth. Contemporary literature became a very small thing in my life for several years, and everyone connected with it. Exactly like Rimbaud, I'd shut the door on it to join another, more electrifying tumult, life itself.

DS: Since then, what directions have you taken as a writer?

BH: A number of beginnings but no resolutions. I want something that hasn't been achieved before. Something entirely different. Something that will expand the untenable.

DS: By something different, what do you mean?

BH: Basically, a totally different concept of the hero. Someone who starts from a completely different standpoint and thinks entirely differently to all the central persons in today's novels and plays, who are all defeated. Like everyone else, I find these characters incestuously derivative and dull. They have killed Literature off stone dead. By comparison, all the excitement has passed to films and television, and this is largely due to the mass media poaching most of the more technically able writers by paying them far more than publishers do.

DS: You say modern literature is a bore. Where did it go wrong?

BH: Briefly, one must judge literature on whether it's creating men who can change the world. The phenomena, the circumstances, the events of our living have become so complex that more and more people are succumbing to nervous breakdowns and all sorts of psychosomatic disorders. The purpose of literature is to create a form of communication that can make men infinitely adaptable and superior to all the complexities of the future. Their master. Now, if this is impossible, then literature is pointless. You can't continue a literature which is concerned merely with comforting and bandaging weak people and creating a false reality when all sorts of terrible things are occurring in life. When these are on one's doorstep, the book one is reading becomes a mockery. Literature has to make Titans, has to be the communication for Titans, or literature is totally obsolescent. It's a pill, a palliative, it's a sedative of consciousness. Today's literature, or the general run of it, is created by people who have defeated themselves. They need the popularity of other cripples. What does fame mean, when you look at all the people who are applauding?

DS: You spoke earlier of Maugham's regrets. How do you think he might respond to literature today were he suddenly to reappear on the scene?

BH: The interesting thing about some of his stories, such as *The Razor's Edge* or *The Moon and Sixpence*, was that he could see out of his window another kind of reality; but if he'd really embraced it in his own work, it would have destroyed the whole fabric of his style. All the characters and situations he wrought, virtually everything. He'd have had to start right back at the beginning. But he couldn't do it. He lacked the vitality. He was caught in too much of the old society. But I do think that if he were to come shooting out of the earth again, he would have a very different understanding of the needs of literature. And of his own, too. I think he was an inherently honest man who never, ever quite fooled himself. He half-fooled himself, but never completely. That was one of the things that made him unhappy. He knew where greatness was, but dared not take a step in that direction. He was absolutely in no doubt that it meant chaos: that terrain does, you know. And really, he was a most fastidious man who disliked chaos enormously. His stutter was a clear signal of that. To him chaos represented self-extinction. But he admired Dostoievsky because he throve on it.

DS: In your concept of what literature should be and should do, where then does greatness lie?

BH: What we want to create, basically, is this: a mind that can set off in a totally new direction and experience. If you, for instance, start a totally different conversation with a person you've never met before, you find the conversation takes a totally new direction from our conversation before. New questions are raised, so there are startling answers that can follow. The same with living. If you live in a different way, you embark on and create different circumstances. But how to solve those different circumstances and problems? We want to create a mind that's a problem solver. That's the man we want to find in the future—one who can set off in new directions, encounter oncoming problems—and solve them. This is what literature is all about. When you create a new mind, you create new responses from people, and they give you responses that you've not encountered before. And you can solve them. You have total confidence in your ability to solve them. Right now what we are doing in literature is creating lives that are a repetition of yesterday and the day before. Well, we didn't solve yesterday or the day before, and we aren't going to solve tomorrow, but we're going to survive it. This is how the old people thought. But now we want to create a new man who can think instantaneously and originally. We want to create man as master of the world. Language, too, is continuing to conceal rather than reveal. Authorities speak but say nothing. Yet so long as they speak, people accept. The sound of words is comforting. Also, I certainly feel that most people who think alike—in our direction anyway—recharge each other. One of the terrible truths of old genius is that generally it was totally isolated. I'm thinking of people like Blake and Van Gogh. One can do a prodigious amount alone, but one always can do more with help. I don't think it's possible to achieve all one's potentialities alone.

DS: Do you have an ideal reader in mind?

BH: No, not really. I think I only write for people of my own imagination. And of course one or two very close friends. But certainly not with the public in mind. I think that literature of the sort that we're thinking of will be very difficult to absorb, and will require a different attitude on the part of the public. It's coming, actually. I have more hope about people now than I had twenty-five years ago. I think more and more people are shunning this manufactured business in the papers, television, and radio. There's already something suspect. I think that's very exhilarating. I think everything is accomplishable now.

DS: I understand that you're working on a play about Christopher Marlowe. How does this project tie in with your notion of a new literature, a new hero?

BH: When you look at Marlowe, you find that he was in fact the beginning of something that could have been another direction. I think, of course, that he was the most important figure of the Elizabethan times. I think he was Shakespeare. I think he was the man who began really the attack on the Church and saw how false it was. The play I am writing about Marlowe is very exciting. It's going to be a complete reversal of everything that most people believe or think about human beings. But one has to stop leading a very comfortable existence mentally. One must learn to be uncomfortable. Shaw said, "There's nothing more cruel than making people think." Once they start thinking, there's no end to it. But suddenly society won't let one be ignorant anymore. And yet, on the other hand people are more and more impervious to the consequences and conclusions of what is happening. More and more people are retreating from the world. This is a very exciting, very interesting period. Most people know that they're being dishonest. I think they know if they're deceiving themselves. I think we're coming to a point now where they're only going to respond to truth. I think truth is exhilarating if one can feed one's own vitality. That's all one needs. Vitality. Fountains of it!

IV
John Wain:
Man of Letters

"Well, this marks the end of a long journey for you." The speaker was British man of letters, John Wain, who at the moment was also loading a basket of clean laundry into the back seat of the family car. His wife, Eirian, sat behind the wheel next to me. A few minutes earlier Wain had met me at the Oxford train station. On this bright warm day on the 23rd of July I was to see firsthand the world of John and all the Wains.

This is not to imply that Wain was a total stranger to me. It seemed that I had been preparing for this meeting ever since 1973, when I happened to pick up and read a copy of his first novel, *Hurry on Down* (1953). Today, after ten novels, eight volumes of verse, many volumes of criticism, and a celebrated biography of Samuel Johnson, Wain is established as a distinguished scholar-artist whose writing attracts a world-wide reading audience.

What I found attractive in the writings, I found confirmed in the individual. In many respects Wain is an 18th century man who upholds the values of tradition, respect, and intellectual honesty. He delights in pointing out that he and Johnson were born in the same district ("the Potteries") and in much the same social milieu; that he attended the same university as Johnson(Oxford); and that he has known, like Johnson, the Grub Street experience and "the unremitting struggle to write enduring books against the background of an unstable existence."

It is not surprising, therefore, to find that the Wains live in an 18th

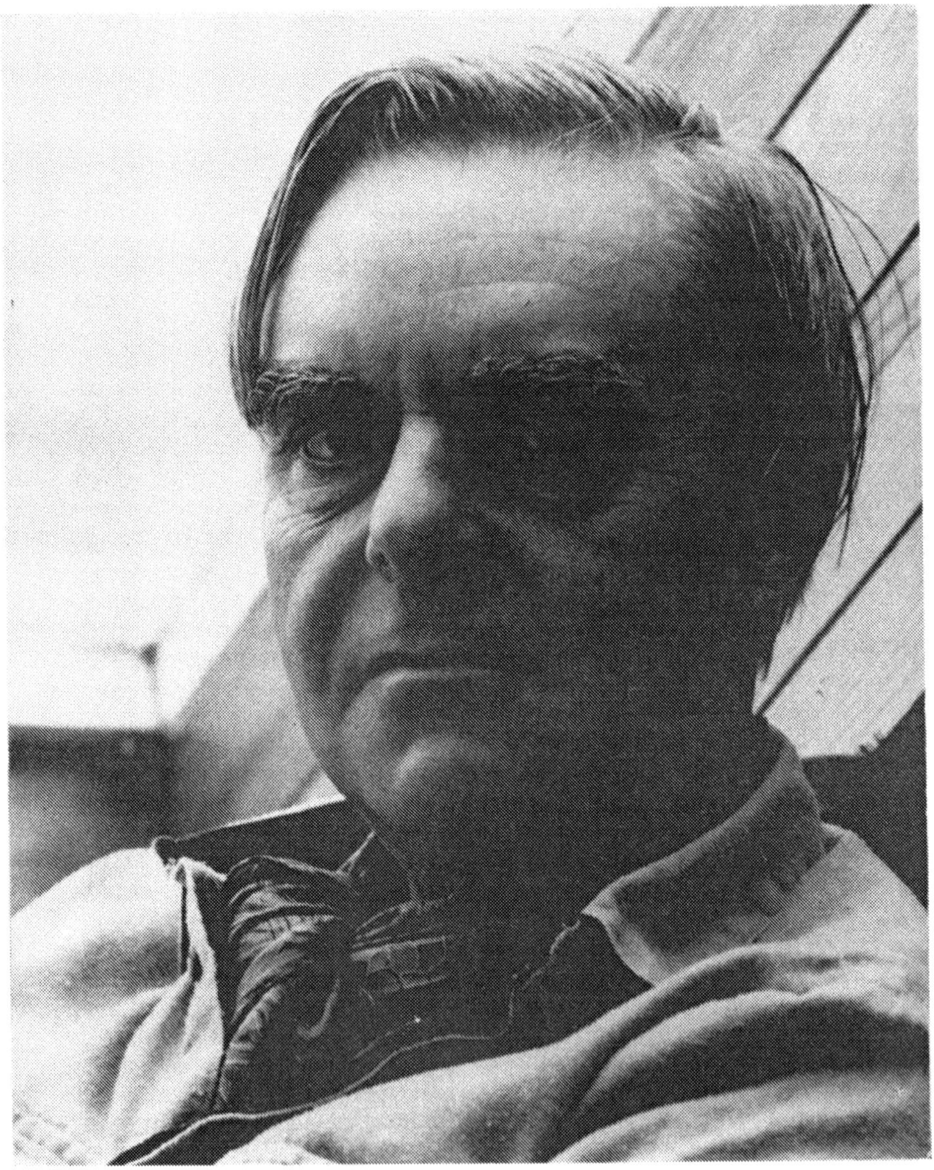

century stone house in Oxford, close to the Thames River. It is a house with a character of its own: a picture of Bohemian disorder. The Wains are unassuming people relaxed with a lifestyle they seem to wish for everybody.

From his cottage we drove past Oxford's ancient colleges to his (and C. S. Lewis') favorite 18th century pub—the Trout Inn. Over a pint of bitter we talked about his years at Oxford—as both student (1943-1946) and Professor of Poetry (1973-1978), and about his college tutor, C. S. Lewis. Through it all, Wain's mind moved effortlessly. There was no sense of the slight uneasiness that one sometimes feels on meeting a stranger.

Later, he invited me to dine with him at Brasenose College. I accepted gladly, and that evening we proceeded to the hall, where I was seated next to him at the high table—in the presence of the grave and reverend worthies of the college. The experience was stimulating—stimulating not through the sober discussion of weighty literary matters, though we had that, but chiefly because of the sheer joy of being with a man of such enormous vitality, and such a generous outgoing spirit to a stranger from across the Atlantic.

More than anything else, I received the impression of Wain as the catalyst, the animating element in the group. At times during the day he looked older than his 55 years. At other times, especially when he had an audience, he looked years younger. His face lit up, he was funny, and he always had something interesting to say.

I shall always remember our first meeting—the warm smile, his *joie de vivre*, his instantaneous outreach to an overseas visitor. Most of all, I shall remember him as a good companion. As he said when we parted late that night: "This shall be an ongoing thing." I look forward to more.

JOHN WAIN

DS: How difficult is it for a serious writer, such as yourself, to make a living from his work in England?

JW: It's more difficult now than it's ever been in my time, because what I have attempted to do for twenty-five years is live on my backlist. I've always had plenty of books in print. The situation has been that every day somebody, somewhere, buys a copy of a book of mine. They may be reordering for a library, or they may be buying a paperback book off a stall, but somebody buys a book somewhere and it just ticks along. Now all of a sudden that's no longer possible, because publishers don't keep the books in print. When I started—and for a good many years afterwards—if a book was published and at the end of ten years it had paid for itself and had made a little profit, everybody was quite happy. But now it has got to pay for itself in one year or else the publisher pulps it. Everything has become much more difficult. The publishers are scared of tying up capital. They must have a return on their capital. What happens now is that while I am writing a new book, I have to live off the advance I get for it. Incidentally, you refer to making a living in England. I never have just made a living in England. You see, another reason that I kept going was that my books were always translated into different languages and sold pretty well all over the world. Now the publishing business is in trouble all over the world, too, and I'm getting far fewer translations and far fewer cheap editions in other countries. So that's more difficult now than it's ever been. I'm not starving. I carry on. I diversify a good deal. I always stick to the principle that I don't do anything for money. I just do the sort of work that I want to do, and then I hope that some money will result from it.

DS: Do you think literary criticism is at all purposeful? Either in general or specifically about your own books? Is it ever instructive?

JW: Well, of course one would have to be mad to say that no valuable criticism exists. Of course, good criticism is of great help. In anything, intelligent comment can come from the people who are not doing the thing but are watching it. The situation that creates intelligent criticism in politics, intelligent criticism in economics—indeed, intelligent criticism of your actions no matter what you are doing—is welcome. Obviously there must be people who are interested in the arts, look at pictures, and listen to music and read books. Because they're interested, they talk about what they've been reading, looking at, or listening to. When they talk, that's criticism. I accept the absolutely basic definition of criticism that I think Frank Kermode gave somewhere when he said, "It is the medium in which past work survives." That would take you all the way from cocktail party chatter to learned academic theses. As long as somebody is paying attention to a work of art, it is surviving. And criticism is absolutely essential.

I personally do not read very much of the criticism that is written about me because I find it rather unsettling. I like thoughtful criticism from people I feel confident with, people I feel are trying to help me to become a better writer. In that respect my friends are very useful to me. They talk to me about my work, and when they are people I trust I don't mind if they point out weaknesses, especially since I've usually seen them myself. I dislike snide, bitchy criticism as I think everybody does. If you read something whose motive quite obviously is just to score off you, to show how much cleverer the critic is than the writer, or possibly even worse, something whose intention is to give pain to you and to your friends, the result is very unsettling. And for that reason I ceased about twenty years ago to read systematically the things that were written about me. Publishers as a rule send a file containing all the reviews of any book. They have one copy for themselves and one for the writer. Well, mine have been under instructions for twenty years not to send me that file. What I find out about what one has said about me is sometimes helpful, sometimes not. On the whole I take it very, very sparingly. I think you've got to be your best critic. The next best thing is somebody who identifies very much with your work, enjoys your work, wants to go on enjoying it, and wants it to be even better. Those are the people who help you.

Apart from that I'd just like to say that I write criticism myself. In cases where I write criticism of living authors I never think of myself writing for the author. I am writing for the prospective reader. If I do a book review, I think of reviewing as a news service. One is writing to tell the reader what new books have come out, what they're like, and whether he would like them if he liked that kind of book. Of course one discusses the merits of the book, but it's not the author I'm writing for. It is the reader. And even in the case of one or two formal studies which I have done of living authors, I have really treated them as if they were classics. I mean, I have done an elaborate essay on Philip Larkin's poetry. I didn't imagine that I was going to make any difference with the way Larkin writes poetry by writing that, but I was helping to get him a more understanding public. I don't think that even his admirers understand quite how good he is. I can perhaps make a difference in his situation by preparing a public to be more intelligent about him. But it's not going to make a difference to anything he's going to do, really.

DS: Today, for the poet, it seems more difficult to get an audience, to get the kind of reception a good writer might have gotten, say, in the 1920s. Even in the 1950s we got a consensus about important writers. Today, however, we don't. Why? Is it because, as Yeats once said, "One thing about we poets, there are too many of us."? Or is it the fault of the critic-reviewer, few of whom really have the authority to make judgments? Or is it something else?

JW: Well, I think you've got a number of things going there that I'd like to sort out. The person under the biggest difficulty at the moment is not the poet but the novelist. Poetry is not in very deep trouble at the moment, given the fact that the poet does not expect a mass public, and that nobody who sets out to write poetry ever expects a mass public. We've settled down into an interesting pattern with poetry in this country, and I think it's very similar in America. The poet reaches his audience primarily through the poetry reading. These are now extremely common. Every town in England has a poetry reading at some time or other. The people in that town who are interested turn out and they listen. Usually the poet's books are on sale either at the back of the hall or down the road at the local bookshop, because the publisher sees to that or should see to that. Poetry has not become an entirely oral art. The printed book is, as it were, the back up. If people like the sound of the poems and think that they'd like to read them at their leisure, they'll get the book. They're not going to go out and buy a book by a poet they've never heard, read, or who doesn't mean anything to them. But it's when they can attach a face to his name and get some sense of identity that they will in fact buy the book. The poet reaches his public now fairly easily, I would say. I don't think there are many poets with the slightest gift who are languishing in complete obscurity, whereas there are a lot of novelists, beginning novelists, with great gifts, who *are* languishing in complete obscurity. This is because the novel has to reach its public through the printed book. The printed book is expensive. For reasons I've just been giving, it's in trouble. I would much rather be a poet just starting out than a novelist just starting out today.

I would just like to say, with regard to contemporary poetry, that certainly in England we happen to have been going through one of those phases where there isn't an overarching genius in the way that T. S. Eliot was accepted as an overarching genius, and then perhaps in later years W. H. Auden was accepted as an overarching genius. Certainly Yeats was the greatest poet in the English speaking world and was accepted as so for the last thirty or forty years before his death. Now, we haven't got one of those. We haven't got an overwhelming presence or even an overwhelming group, really. There are a lot of poets doing interesting work, but nobody is particularly dominant. Occasionally some pressure group tries to put forward somebody as the poet of the day, but it never sticks for very long. I don't think this situation is very strange, for we had an exactly similar period in English literature between 1750 and 1800. In the second half of the 18th century a lot of very interesting poets were writing, but you can't look back and say there is one dominant poet. On the other hand, you could look a little bit earlier and point to Pope, or you could look a little bit further ahead and point to Wordsworth and Coleridge. In that period of almost half a century, or more than half a century, there are interesting poets but no dominant poet. I should say that's about how we are now. The reason that there isn't a consensus about who the big poets are is, if anything, attributable to people's common sense.

DS: Has your conception of what literature is and ought to be changed much since the 1950s?

JW: Well, have I got a conception of what literature is and ought to be? I don't think I've got any sort of particularly prescriptive definition of what it ought to be. I think that all imaginative artists work in the medium that they happen to be drawn to. If I were a painter, it would be colors and shapes and so on. If I were a musician, it would be sounds. But since I am a writer, it's words. I think that you gain what illumination you can about life and you pass it on in the appropriate medium. I don't think I've ever thought anything different. I have never at any time thought that self-expression is what it was about. I've never written to express myself. I have seen the statement occasionally from writers that they're interested in self-expression, total self-expression. It may be that their reasoning is that there's only one human heart that they have known absolutely in depth and that's their own, and if they lay that bare it's going to be true for other people, too. That may be the reasoning. In my case, I think I've always in varying ways tried to understand other people. I try to have the kind of imagination that goes out to other people and comprehends their lives. Of course, one does express one's self, and that's one reason why there's no need to make a program of it. I think if you invent something, the mere fact that you invent that story and not some other, the mere fact that you write about people of a certain kind and not some other—all these things tell a great deal about yourself. And I know that sometimes when I look back at something I wrote years ago, it seems to me to reflect perfectly my situation at that time, yet I didn't write it to express my situation. So, all I can say is that I think literature is an imaginative art by which I believe very much that it means comprehending other people, having sympathy generally with the creation, including animals, of course. And you do it as well as you can and with as little falsification as you can, with no self-indulgent tricks of style which you're putting in to show that you're clever. You do it as decently as you can and the result, if it's good enough, is literature. I don't think I've thought anything else, but you know I very, very rarely have verbalized it. This must be one of the first times I've ever actually made a general statement like that, but that's what I think.

DS: It's one thing to be identified as a particular kind of writer, another to be identified with a particular group. How did you feel in the 1950s about being labelled a so-called Angry Young Man, and how do you feel about it today?

JW: I'm not even very happy about being identified as a certain type of writer, because I think that one ought always to have the right to do something quite different and not get type cast. Actors often break a successful career to do something else because they don't want to be type cast. When I have asked myself what use I am to the world as a writer, or what is the best way I can work, it has always seemed to me that the best thing I can do is to write a book that only I could write. Or write a poem or a story that only I could write. Not because I am important. As I've said before, I don't write for self-expression. But because my individuality is the contribution I can make. My individuality is the instrument that I can use. And if I tried to write like someone else because I thought that would be a good selling line, well, it's unthinkable to do any such thing. That is what the popular writer does. What a serious writer does is to say he will write a book that only he could write. Now, I have always tried to do that. I have felt it irksome that I have so often been bracketed with other writers, stuck to other writers—very often with people that I haven't seen very much similarity with. I think the reason is partly that we live in the age of the journalist. With the best will in the world—some of them are very decent people—they see things in a journalistic way. They like to make generalizations. They like to talk about groups. When a book is published, it becomes a success and gets talked about (if it is talked about) on television and on the radio, and sometimes in the papers. Now basically, all the people who do that are journalists. Very often they don't understand with the best will in the world that literature is just not interesting in their way. They always want to make a news story of it or they want to make a movement. When John Osborne had a success with *Look Back in Anger* in 1956, the critics and newspaper columnists wanted some of the names to go with it. They don't like just mentioning one name. They like to have a movement. They look around, they found people, jammed us together, and we became the Angry Young Men. I have always found it rather irksome. It's never helped me. I try to not be resentful about it because it's a waste of one's effort, but

I have always hoped that ultimately I would win through to a public who read me because I was me.

DS: When you write, do you have an ideal audience in mind?

JW: It's very difficult, that one. One's thinking and feeling are not absolutely consistent there. Writing is not a completely homogeneous thing. If I sit down to work at 8:30 in the morning and work until 12:30, it's not like a dynamo going in a smooth way. There is a moment when you're really creating something, when you're really getting the next ideas. Supposing you're writing a novel. There's a moment when you get an idea of the next bit of story. Or you're inventing dialogue and you invent what the person is going to say, what the next person is going to say the next time, and so on. Those are the moments when you are really creating, and they never last for more than a few seconds at a time. Then you're polishing and rearranging, and you're implementing the idea you've just had, and some of that is quite low tension. You get up close to it, then you stand back from it. Writing is very much a hill and dale thing. Now, at the moments of white heat you're not thinking of anybody else. You're too jammed up against your material. There isn't room between you and the material for the thought of anybody else. Other times, you tend to have a sense of the kind of person you would like to be interested in what you are writing. And indeed, sometimes I think of actual people. I think, oh, that would amuse so and so. I think of my readers as more or less similar people to the ones that I actually do know—various friends who like my work. Sometimes I think quite concretely about them. At other times, when one is surging forward again, the thought of anybody else is blotted out by the closeness up to the work.

The other thing is this: whether or not we think about a specific public, all of us are very socially conditioned. We all tend to spend our time with people of a certain kind. In my case, the people I naturally hang around with are the professional middle class of my country, of Western Europe, and of America. I mean, the sort of people that I instinctively understand are people in the sort of job that my family and friends tend to be in—academic professions, law, medicine, journalism. They make decisions, they have responsible jobs, they also have an interest in the arts and ideas. While I do know people who come from right outside those categories, my social expectation is that I shall spend most of my time with such people. That goes very deep. If I wanted to write for a proletarian audience, for example, well, I would just write the sort of thing I write normally and hope that they would like it. I couldn't write down to them or up to them or anything else. They're just people. But my natural idiom is the idiom of the people I live among, and these are really the audience you think of.

DS: Concerning *Strike the Father Dead*, am I correct in assuming that Bill Coleman—whose career you celebrate in *Letters to Five Artists*—was the inspiration behind the character, Percy Brett?

JW: The whole way that that was worked out is really most interesting. I have always admired Bill Coleman. When I was a schoolboy—about 1940—I had some of his records. I never of course realized that I would ever meet him or anything of that kind. I just admired him very much. Years went by. I grew up into my thirties, and then I decided to write a novel about somebody who becomes a jazz musician. I called the hero "Coleman." Now, as a matter of fact my conscious reason was that I wanted a very English name. The hero's father is a professor, and he comes from a kind of middle-class professional English family. I wanted a name that would be a very English name. Of course, I realize now that there must have been something deeper going on. I must have been thinking deep down of Bill Coleman. Then I came to do this portrait of this black American horn player who opts to live in Paris. Now, of course, I did know that Bill Coleman is the diagram of that sort of person. I mean a lot of black jazz musicians have done that, but he's the one who has done it most successfully. He adapted to France most successfully. He spent the 1930s there and then he had to go home during the war. Then he came back straightaway after the war, and Paris is his home. And he's married to a Swiss lady.

The bits of the book that he comes in are not very long and didn't take very long to write. I can't really remember what I thought while I was doing that. I was writing the book in Italy. But I do know that if you had said to me, "Now is there anybody in real life who is like this?" I would have said, "Well, that's what Bill Coleman and people like that must be like." I must have thought of it. And of course in 1962 the book was published in French. The publisher gave a party in Paris and some genius in the office thought of asking Bill Coleman. He came, I got to know him, and we got to be very close. He is a very important person in my life. I love him very much and I admire him very much. That was a wonderful thing that that person did for me who scribbled his name down on that list.

So Percy Brett is not a portrait of Bill Coleman. As a matter of fact, I never have attempted a portrait of him. My poem about him and Django Reinhardt has a different field of reference. One of the subjects that interests me most is history in its broad sense. I think that we are where we are as a result of a journey. Every nation and every individual came from somewhere. I am always very interested to know what journeys people have had and where they've been and how they wound up where they are. Those wonderful jazz recordings that were made by Django Reinhardt and Bill Coleman in Paris before the war—one a gypsy, another a black man—with Hitler's armies just poised to roll in, and wedded to the doctrine that both of those were inferior races who were going to have to be stamped out. Paris in all its brilliance in that moment just before the war was reflected in that marvelous jazz of these two people. It is such a wonderful piece of history, that that's really an historical poem. I mean, it's got a little portrait of Bill—what he looks like and what he sounds like—but it's really starting with the slave ships and the caravans and then the two of them meeting. So while I have written a lot about Bill, I haven't ever really given a portrait of him.

DS: Could you say something about the starting point, the genesis, of *The Smaller Sky* and *The Young Visitors*?

JW: I can't say anything about the genesis of *The Smaller Sky*. I was having a drink in a pub in Kensington and I was talking to Rosemary Tonks, a friend of mine. All of a sudden, not apropos of anything, I had this marvelous idea for the man who won't go off the railway station. It had nothing to do with anything my friend was saying. It had nothing to do with anything in the situation at all. I was just having a sociable drink and suddenly I got this idea for a novel. I didn't at that moment know why, but I knew I had to write that book. And I went home and I wrote it very quickly. I mean, usually it takes me a very long time, but I think I wrote that in about two months. Now that was just an idea, just a *donnee*.

The Young Visitors was another matter. I had spent some time in Russia and reacted unfavorably to it. I didn't like the atmosphere. Before I went I was sentimental about Russia, ready to believe anything that people told me about how it was getting more democratic. When I got there, I just couldn't take it. I didn't like the endless brainwashing that people were doing. And some of the young visitors who were detailed to show me and my wife around were *komsomol* kids, all handpicked. I found these kids pretty insufferable. I'm always a bit suspicious of young people who are too obedient to their elders anyway, but these people had swallowed the line so totally that I found them rather irritating. I conceived the notion of a visit to England by a gang of these kids and what happens to them. After that it was just making up a story, because I did want to have a kind of Romeo and Juliet story. They meet what I hope isn't a typical Western socialist, because he's phony, but they meet the sort of rather self-indulgent socialist that we do tend to get who's always singing the praises of the Soviet system, but would do anything in effect but actually go there. They fall in love across this ideological barrier and then they really are in love. Then they're dragged apart like Romeo and Juliet in the end. I've said a number of things I wanted to say, but the genesis of it was just feeling irritated with those komsomol young people.

DS: I know of your closeness to the people and country of Wales. It was a long time, however, before you dared write *A Winter in the Hills*.

JW: Well, yes, it was. Wales has always been an important country to me. As a child my holidays were in Wales because it was the nearest bit of sea coast to where I grew up. It's always meant a country that's been very beautiful and restoring. Wales has been a kindly foster mother to me. But it wasn't until I got married to a Welsh woman—when I was thirty-four years old—that I really bought the package, as it were. If you marry somebody of a certain nationality, you just marry that nation. And I was thrown into a situation where I was very often in places and among people that I would have just not got in or among as an English visitor. And I started thinking how fascinating it would be to write about them. I started to do the book in 1968 or maybe the last week or two of 1967, but I wrote the book basically in 1968, and finished it in February, 1969. So it did take me eight years. I mean it took me eight years to work up the nerve. On the whole the view that I had of the North Welsh people—there is a North-South difference in every country and these are North Welsh I'm writing about—is just about what I still do have. In other words, if my present view is right, then I would say I had it right in 1968. But in writing the book I went through a number of stages. First of all, I was sentimental about them and didn't see any fault in them at all. In fact, those certain passages of a first draft I threw out because they were too sentimental. So that I was, as it were, adjusting even during the writing of the book.

DS: *The Pardoner's Tale*, technically speaking, seems to be a departure for you, in that it is a novel-within-a-novel. Would you comment on that?

JW: The temptation to write a novel about a novelist is always there with any of us. I mean, the thought processes of a novelist are interesting, and sooner or later a lot of novelists write a novel about a novelist. I'm also interested in narrative. I think narrative is a wonderful art. I think nothing shows the mistaken basis of a lot of modern literary opinion than the way they have a contempt for narrative. I think narrative is immensely important. All the great writers have been great storytellers, and the greatest critic of all, Aristotle, made it the most important thing in the *Poetics*. Now I wanted to tell a story. In writing a novel about a man who is writing a novel, I wanted to take him over the months that it takes him to do the book and to describe what happens in his life during those months. Then gradually towards the end the two narratives begin to affect one another to some extent. I think it's just an interesting device. I can say certain things I want to say about life and about creativity. I mean, it's really about two things: it's about the problems of the flesh, and it's about creativity. They're both very real problems, very real issues, and I just ran the two together. That seemed to be the way to do it. I don't know what else. The critic takes over after that and says anything else about it, but that's what I thought I'd do.

DS: In some respects *The Pardoner's Tale* is a painfully sad story. Should one necessarily take it as your last word on marriage, creativity, art, life, and so forth?

JW: No, no. It's not my last word. It is a sad, somber book in some ways, but there again, you see, the novel that Giles writes has two alternative endings. When his personal life seems to be going right and he gets what he thinks of as a new lease on life—with his relationship with the young lady—he writes a very happy ending. Then life actually gives him a shakedown and he realizes it's not going to happen. So he writes a depressed ending. But I did leave the two endings. It's just as likely or as unlikely that one might happen as the other. I'm not trying to make a final statement. I'm trying to say that in the bewildering richness of life, this can happen and that can happen—all sorts of things can happen. What I suppose it does say in the end is that all these problems are fundamental to people and everybody has them.

DS: *Samuel Johnson*, your masterpiece—so acclaimed by many reviewers—draws from thirty years of experience as a reader, writer, scholar. How did you know when it was time to begin the actual writing of that biography?

JW: I had a friendly push from an agent, and I have to say that. I'd been going about for years saying that one of these days I shall write a book on Johnson. And I vaguely thought that I'd do it in my old age.

I thought it might be the thing that I would do in my declining years. I would put together all the thought that I had had about Johnson. But then my American agent at the time—John Cushman, now with a different firm but still a good friend of mine—heard me talk about Johnson. He said, "Why don't you just write down on a couple of sheets of paper the sort of book you would write if you wrote your book on Johnson. What would it be like?" So just to oblige him, I did. He showed it to a publisher and he came back with a very good offer and he fixed it. He did what a good agent should do. Your agent should be rather like a boxer's manager. Your agent knows you and he knows the situation in the field. He says my boy's ready for that fight now. It was really John Cushman's idea.

DS: Could you tell me something about your methods of working? Do you have an established routine?

JW: Well, I have established hours. When I can I like to start working early in the morning. My brain is fresh and I like to, if I can, be left undisturbed. I like to start working at about eight in the morning and work until about mid-day, and then anybody can have the rest of the day. I get all of the other things done. Sometimes I work again between tea and dinner, between 4:30 and 7:00. But usually the work I do then is not quite so intensive. It might consist of revision or something of that sort. Sometimes I need to be sitting and typing, because the ideas are coming too fast for me to write them down in longhand. Other times I write very slowly. Still other times I stand up. I have a stand-up desk. Then sometimes I like to sit in an armchair. The physical means of writing are very important to me. For instance, I could never dictate. I have to have the physical feeling of transmitting words. I couldn't just spit them into the air. I have to engrave them somehow. Which is what a lot of writers have said.

Apart from that, what else? Nothing. As for poetry, I have no working method. A poem just comes. I might say that for the next six months I will be working on this book. I never say that for the next six months I will be going on with poetry, though I might in fact write quite a lot in those six months. It just comes when it comes. It can come riding home on the train late at night, or shaving. Anything. If I am writing fiction, I write out a draft. I'm a very slow worker. I try when writing fiction to write 3000 words a week. If you could do 3000 words a week you could write a novel in a year. You would do 12,000 a month and that would be 96,000 in eight months. That would allow for holidays and having influenza and so on. And yet, I have never done that. 3000 words is not much. It's only twelve pages of typescript double-spacing, but in fact I can do 3000 in one week, 6000 in two, 9000 in three. I can do 12,000 in four weeks, and then I dry up and I have to do something else. I can't keep it up at that pace, and so that is one reason I diversify so much. I have to have a rest from what I am doing.

DS: May I ask what you are working on at the moment?

JW: At the moment I am writing a novel for young people, and a play, and I've got a serious novel waiting which I'm ready to start at any moment. But since I've got two things going already, I won't add a third just yet. Then there are always occasional jobs, of course. One writes an occasional article or something of that sort.

DS: What is the subject of the play you are writing?

JW: The play is entitled *Frank* and it's about Frank Barber—servant to Samuel Johnson. If I can't get it put on as a play I shall make an historical novel of it, which would be very much a departure for me. My novels have always been set in what was the present moment when I wrote them. I look at the world I see going on around me and I write about what is right there in front of me. I never go backward or forward in time. This would be a play set in the eighteenth century, but I think it would avoid all the trappings. I have made them talk like modern people. I wouldn't make any attempt to represent eighteenth century English or anything. The issues which are about freedom and servitude are perennial issues and are just as alive now as in the days of the formal slave trade. I certainly don't think that slavery has ever died out. It may have died out in name, but the actual *thing* is still very much with us.

DS: May we close with a statement of what motivates you as a writer?

JW: Well, you could invent all sorts of high-flown answers to that, but the fact is basically that if you are a writer you write. If you are a painter, you paint. If you are a musician, you produce music. That's the kind of animal that God made you. Being a writer is not a profession. It's a condition. And that's the condition that I'm in. If anything happens to stop me writing for more than a week or two at a time, I get very neurotic. My life is entirely styled toward expressing myself through the written word. I just get very ill if I don't do it, that's all.

V
Colin Wilson:
The Man Behind the Outsider

When I began preparing for my interview with British philosopher-novelist Colin Wilson, over forty books containing more than six million words confronted me—sufficient material for several years of reading, at least. The task of preparing was further compounded by Wilson's ranging eclecticism. At thirteen he had already written an essay called "Questions on the Life Aim," raising the problems: "Why are we alive? What are we supposed to do now we are here?" Ten years later he sketched out a book considering the answers of the major thinkers of the 19th and 20th centuries—the great "outsider" figures from Kierkegaard to T. E. Hulme and Gurdjieff. *The Outsider*, published when he was twenty-four, brought him overnight fame and was translated into twenty-two languages. This instant success brought an equally violent reaction: "I suddenly became the world's most unpopular writer."

Since *The Outsider*, he has written philosophical treatises, books on the occult, novels, an autobiography, collections of essays, and even an encyclopedia of murder—in which he records case histories of many famous murderers, and illustrates his own preoccupation with psychology of violence.

With so much material before me, there was nothing to do but plunge, so plunge I did. After weeks of reading and rereading, patterns began to surface: areas of prolonged interest and deep concern emerged. These patterns and areas became the basis of our discussions.

We first met at the Curzon Hotel, Hyde Park, where Wilson was staying with the compliments of film producer, Dino De Laurentiis, for whom he was revising a movie script. At 49, Wilson looked bland, self-assured, and younger than his age—too young yet to be a grand old man of English letters, but a considerable literary presence all the same. Like Gore Vidal, he has usually been good newspaper copy, not afraid to be quoted on, for instance, the need for privacy: "It's tremendously important to work alone, to be capable of standing alone," he said. He paused, frowned, and then added: "A very tiny proportion of human beings doesn't need an audience."

What seemed at first casual was often his remarkable ease with himself and his beliefs. "My aim has always been the same," said Wilson—with the patient but slightly pained air of one whose works have often been misunderstood. "My books are about those sudden flashes of absolute happiness and certainty, the feeling that there is meaning in the world." Wilson is deeply interested in those strange moments in which we get the curious feeling that somehow, what is, is intended. The trouble with most human beings, continued Wilson, is that we know we're trapped in the here and now, and we have allowed ourselves to be defeated by the here and now. "If we have any sense of a destiny, we won't waste our time wandering around and doing nothing or feeling sorry for ourselves, but go straight for the object."

And to people who accuse him of being arrogant, aloof, he cites what Beatrice Webb once said about George Bernard Shaw: "'He was like a cat. He liked people that he really knew well.' I tend to be the same kind of person myself."

COLIN WILSON

DS: Is it difficult for you as a serious writer to make a living in England?

CW: It was difficult in 1956 when *The Outsider* came out. That book made a fair amount of money because it sold very well here and in the United States and went into about sixteen different languages in its first year. Nevertheless, the money it made—about 16,000 pounds, a lot then—went fairly quickly because of income tax and because when you change your style of living you begin to spend a lot of money. The second book, *Religion and the Rebel*, was attacked violently by the critics who said it had been a mistake ever to have praised *The Outsider*. As a consequence, although the second book sold moderately well, it didn't make much money by comparison. From then on for the next few years I was very broke. We moved to Cornwall in 1957 to escape all the publicity that the Angry Young Men were getting. We were extremely broke. In fact, we used every penny we had to move into the house. Then we just had to borrow some money on the same mortgage even to afford any furniture. In those days I didn't realize that you could have an overdraft at the bank. And so for months after we moved into the house we just had no cash at all until my novel *Ritual in the Dark* was accepted by Victor Gollancz—who had done *The Outsider*. In America, it was accepted by Houghton Mifflin, who gave me, I think, a $5,000 advance which they didn't recover for years. *Ritual in the Dark* was sort of a moderate success. But it was still a matter of being broke all the time and going to America to do lecture tours to make a little money. I did my first tour in 1961, then came back to England, having just paid all my debts, but with no money.

Things didn't begin to improve until the early 1970s, when *The Occult* came out, and that to my surprise made quite a lot of money. A year or two afterwards I was surprised to find that we were still getting checks for about $10,000 a year from America. But writers don't make a lot of money. I still spend half the year living off an overdraft. What I've got going for me now, I suppose, is the fact that my books are in about twenty or thirty languages. Little bits keep dribbling in from all over the place. A new paperback or new edition brings in a few hundred dollars or pounds. This is the kind of thing that basically keeps me going. Of course, doing things like movie scripts helps, too. And so I suppose I tend to live this way, always with the hope that one of these days something will happen to enable me to make enough money to stop me from running so hard.

DS: Your admiration for Shaw is well-known. Do you regret never having met the man? What do you suppose would have come out of such a meeting?

CW: No, very little, because Shaw died in 1951 when I was only just twenty. The only way I might have got to know Shaw and had something to say to him was after *The Outsider* came out. Then I think we'd have had a great deal to say to one another. Shaw was apparently a very nice man. I knew several friends of his later, and they all said that Shaw was the sort of person who needed to get to know you before he'd accept you. Beatrice Webb once said, "He was like a cat. He liked the people that he really knew well." I tend to be the same kind of person myself.

DS: You and Bill Hopkins have been friends for over thirty years.

CW: Bill and I have always been very close. It was Bill's misfortune to arrive with his first book, *The Divine and the Decay*, after *The Outsider* came out. One of the newspapers said Bill Hopkins is the man Wilson is always proclaiming as the only other genius in the world. Well naturally, the result was that when his first novel appeared, the critics attacked it. To have your first book so completely and viciously savaged must be a very nasty experience. But it was due to Bill, really, that I wrote *The Outsider*. I was working in a coffee house and Bill came to visit me one night. We were strolling along the embankment—just past Charing Cross Station—and I was talking to him about my work-in-progress, *Ritual in the Dark*. I was saying that there were three types of outsider. The hero is the intellectual outsider—he knows the discipline of the intellect but not of his emotions or body. The emotional outsider is like Van Gogh. He has discipline of the emotions but not of the intellect or body. And Austin, who is sort of a Nijinsky character, has discipline of the body but not of the intellect or emotions. I felt the most important by far was to have discipline of the intellect. All that I hadn't thought out. It came spontaneously as I was talking to Bill. And then I thought, that would make the basis for a good book. That was towards Christmas in 1954. Over Christmas when I was on my own I started sketching notes for this new book called at that time *The Outsider in Literature*. It was based upon that concept of the three different types of discipline.

DS: Why was *Ritual in the Dark* such a long time coming?

CW: Because when I'd written *The Outsider*, I then submitted *Ritual in the Dark*, first of all to an agent, Curtis Brown, who hated it. Then I submitted it to another publisher, Fred Warburg, who didn't much like it. I must admit that in that early version—based on *The Egyptian Book of the Dead*—it was much more like a constipated James Joycean sort of novel. Eventually I decided that it had to have a story and flow from beginning to end. I settled down and wrote the second version in about 1958. Again, Bill gave me the key to that when I'd been trying again and again to get the right beginning. Joy, my wife, and I met Bill in Hamburg and he just happened to comment about Diaghilev and this perfume *Mitsouka* he always used. He said casually, "Why don't you start the book in the Diaghilev Exhibition?" There had just been a big exhibition in London. I'd seen it seven times. And it was just the right beginning. So I started the book from scratch. This time I went straight through from beginning to end in one sweep.

DS: Considering the attacks in the press and the lack of privacy, the

1950s must have been a discouraging time for you.

CW: No matter how much I was attacked in the 1950s, no matter how discouraging this was, I was forced to write because I needed the money. At that time people were literally breaking into my room and stealing my diaries (they turned up later at the University of Texas). I had absolutely no privacy whatsoever. I had to leave London. It was an absurd situation. There was nothing quite like it in America, simply because when Kerouac and Alan Ginsburg and all of the rest of the Beat generation broke through in 1957, they weren't all in the same place. They were scattered all over America. Whereas at the time, when this happened in England, we were all together in London, except Amis, who was in Swansea. The result was that it really looked like a completely new generation all arriving at the same time with a terrific boom. It would be very difficult to try to describe the kind of nonstop journalism that appeared about us. The number of interviews, the number of times we appeared on television and radio, were enormous. I can understand why people got a big sick of it.

DS: How did the horsewhipping story develop?

CW: Well, it all developed from the fact that Joy's sister had seen my diaries. I had been to see Joy when she was ill in the hospital, having had her tonsils out. I left my diaries around. Her sister Fay came from work and took them and read great chunks of them. A few days later Joy staggered back from a weekend at home, absolutely miserable and exhausted because her family had nagged her all weekend about me. I was so angry about this that when her sister rang up, I said, "If your parents don't stop nagging Joy, I'm going to tell her not to come home for weekends." And this was the last straw. Fay told her parents: "Well, I've read his diaries, and he's a sexual pervert. It's full of sex." So Joy's parents came into my room in Notting Hill, accused me of being a homosexual and having six mistresses, and tried to drag Joy away. The mother hit me on the head with an umbrella and then her father tried to hit me with a horsewhip. Then they tried to drag her away—her parents tugging on one arm and me tugging on the other. I didn't hit her father. I pushed him in the chest to keep him away. He fell down, whereupon her mother started hitting me with the umbrella, saying, "How dare you hit an old man!" And it just struck me as so funny, I was screeching with laughter and actually rolled on the floor. Finally, I managed to ring the police. They came along and said, "How old are you?" She said, "Twenty-one," and they said to her parents, "Well, she's free to do what she likes. We can't do anything about it." As soon as they'd gone, the press arrived, alerted by a guest who'd been having dinner with us. So we fled to Devon, then to Ireland, pursued by the national press. Typically, the newspapers carried the story for weeks. And, of course, that was the worst kind of publicity.

Both Bill Hopkins and I have encountered terrific hostility from the press, which still continues to some extent. It's not as bad now as it was, simply because I've been almost an unknown for fifteen years. In effect I was forgotten in the 1960s. I continue to publish books. I continue to get reviewed, but in a way a lot of people assumed that I was merely repeating *The Outsider* and that I was written out. The result was that, in a way, I vanished. It's only in the past few years that there's a sort of audience coming back and actually finding or discovering me through my books and by word of mouth. Which is probably the right way to do it.

DS: Turning to your subsequent works, *Religion and the Rebel*, *The Stature of Man*, *The Strength to Dream*, *Origins of the Sexual Impulse*, and *Beyond the Outsider* all concern the problem of the outsider. Can you define your ultimate aim in these books?

CW: My aim has always been the same. I said in *Mysteries* that there are two kinds of writers—hedgehogs and foxes. And I quoted Isaiah Berlin: "The fox knows many things, the hedgehog knows only one." Shakespeare was a fox and Tolstoi was a hedgehog. Well, I'm a hedgehog. I know only one thing, and all of my work is about this in one way or another. The one thing I know, or the one thing I've always been wanting to investigate, is the question of those sudden flashes of absolute happiness and certainty. The kind of thing that happens to Meursault at the end of Camus' *L'Etranger*, when he grasps the priest by the throat and suddenly feels himself washed clean and full of an immense happiness. Suddenly he realizes, "I've been happy and I was happy still." These curiously mystical moments, you could almost say, are another mode of consciousness quite unlike our normal mode. In some strange way it lies right alongside our normal mode. It's *not* a mile away from it. You can go into it quite spontaneously at a second's notice.

It's what Proust experienced when he tasted the biscuit dipped in tea. Proust wrote, "I had ceased to feel mediocre, accidental, mortal." And that's the important thing—that sudden feeling of no longer being mediocre and no longer being accidental. These strange moments in which we get the curious feeling that somehow, what is, is intended. This is how life was supposed to be. We have a destiny, and we're working out that destiny. If we have any sense we won't waste our time wandering around and doing nothing or feeling sorry for ourselves, but go straight for the object. All my books are really about that.

DS: What do you feel to be wrong with most human beings? With the way most people live their lives?

CW: Basically I say that we are trapped in the here and now, and that we have allowed ourselves to be defeated by the here and now. Or, we've allowed all sense of direction to be taken away from us. Here's an illustration I've often used: it is like somebody who goes into a room to get something and then forgets what he's gone there for, and says, "Why the hell did I come in here?" We appear to be like this all the time on earth. Sort of scratching our heads and saying, "Why the hell did I come here?" And then it happens—in these curious flashes of the "other mode," you say, "Of *course!*" And it's that "*of course*" that fascinates me.

DS: You explore this human weakness in both The Mind Parasites and The Sex Diary of Gerard Sorme.

CW: The mind parasite is just a symbol for what I call in The Outsider "original sin." That is to say, a symbol for this curious element of weakness in human beings. In The Sex Diary of Gerard Sorme, I said, "Human beings are like grandfather clocks driven by watch springs." There is something wrong. I've said this in book after book. We're like clocks who have hands but whose hands are slightly loose. They never show the right time. Or something silly and very minor like that. All you have to do is tighten up the handles. D. H. Lawrence and all the rest of them seem to think one shouldn't drift. Give way to intuitions. My deep feeling is that there's something wrong with this. Be sure of what you want to do, and do it. So for example, on a long train journey I say to myself, "Okay. I want to get some serious thinking and reading done during this journey. I don't want to feel sleepy." And I get to my destination without feeling sleepy. Ten years ago I'd get there sort of tired out or fed up, simply because I let myself go. So obviously we are always allowing ourselves to be bullied by our misery and exhaustion. With a real effort of will we could do all kinds of interesting things with consciousness. But at the moment this is completely foreign to human nature. Apes and cows wouldn't dream of doing it. They obviously live according to their feelings. We're advancing into a completely new evolutionary field.

DS: Does this revolution have anything to do with the right and left brain experiments?

CW: This seems to me a very important idea. What has happened is that we've developed faculties miles beyond the animals. You could say that as conscious beings we have developed three major components—these being the left cerebral hemisphere, the right cerebral hemisphere, and what I call the "robot" who lives apparently in the cerebellum. The lowest animals, of course, have just one brain, so to speak. The lowest animals have what you might call a robot—something that will do the learning for them and pick it up, store it in memory, and then do it automatically. But what is happening to man is rather curious. The components are, unfortunately, interfering with one another. It is rather like having a car with the brake, accelerator, and clutch so close together that when you try to put your foot on one you put your foot on the other and produce the opposite effect. We have basically developed a kind of close-up perception of the world, a microscope in the left brain which enables us to cope with reality more precisely and ruthlessly than any animal. Second, we have a more efficient robot than any other animal. Our robot will store far more than any other animal's robot will, and will regurgitate it when we need it. Our brain has this enormous capacity.

The strange thing is that in split brain experiments, in which scientists split the brain down the middle so that the two hemispheres are separated, it's revealed that we have two people literally living within our heads. In poltergeist cases, for example, quite obviously it's the right brain which causes object to fly around the room, and yet the child who is responsible never knows that he is responsible. Now, if we knew that this other person was living in our head, and what's more that he was there to support us, it would be marvelous. Then you'd suddenly possess real power. At the moment there's a sort of close alliance between the left brain—the logical half of it—and the robot, and the robot is pushing the right brain into the background. The trouble is that the right brain knows far more than the left does, so we're wasting a huge part of our capacities.

DS: In *The Black Room* you explore the possibility of separating one's self from the physical world and entering totally the world of the mind. How close have you come to reaching that ideal state?

CW: Well, this is a very interesting question. This peculiar power—not just to visualize but to enter your own interior world—should be very simple. But it depends upon not being overly anxious. In other words, not letting your left brain have the last word. Once you've relaxed into a state of serenity, it's not too difficult to do. You can actually close your eyes and visualize things with great clarity. You can conjure up past emotions or feelings and all kinds of things. But you have to do it first of all by going into a peculiarly relaxed state. It can even be a tense state as in Hemingway during the war—when in "Soldier's Home" Krebbs remembers those moments during the war when, under crisis, he suddenly did the one thing, the only thing, and it always came out right. But nevertheless, whichever of the two states it is, it is a state in which the two halves of the brain are completely combined. To some extent I've learned to do this. I've learned to do it by what I think is the right route—by coming to trust my intellect more and more. Dante says, in the third canto, "Who are all these people around here in hell?" And Virgil replies, "They are people who have lost the good of intellect." Dante knew that intellect was good. It's only men like Whitman and Lawrence who think it's bad. My feeling is that I'd rather trust my intellect on the whole than my emotions. We spend half our time being bullied by our emotions and our intuitions and our bodies. But it is possible to get into a state in which you can become the master. Under hypnosis I'm convinced that the left brain goes to sleep. The right remains wide awake. And the right can do far more extraordinary things—under hypnosis—than you could if you told it to. This is because the right brain has the power. So why doesn't it do it when you tell it to? Because it doesn't believe you. It sort of knows that you are a weakling. Now the only way that you are going to get it to do it is by gradually saying, "Look, I'm the boss. And you do what I tell you." And eventually, if you do it long enough, it will do what you tell it.

DS: What would you say is the fundamental difference between your thinking and that of Sartre and Camus?

CW: It seems to me that the existentialism of Sartre and Camus is quite fundamentally mistaken. Sartre in a way was a genuine Communist materialist long before he became a Communist. That is to say, the Communist point of view, the materialist point of view is that we're born into the world because we're biological accidents. There is no kind of meaning outside us. No religion or anything. Now this means in effect that human beings are *reading* meanings into the world. Which implies that the world is totally meaningless. According to Sartre, when you see this meaninglessness it's called *nausea*. But this is a basic error in Sartre's thinking. It doesn't take into account the fact that consciousness is always intentional, so that if you see something as meaningless, you're still *imposing* meaninglessness on it. I am basically an existentialist, which means that I don't take any point of view for granted—certainly not, let's say, the religious position. But I do feel that if you start from a completely existential point of view—that is, you're going to take nothing for granted—you still end up with the sense that meaning is an external datum. Meaning exists outside us. And therefore, in some sense the religious position is true and the materialist position is not true.

My "new existentialism" is, in other words, the important first step to asking the next question. And that is, if meaning exists externally to us, it means that we can make some kind of meaningful effort towards grabbing it, towards grasping it. In that case, how do we do it? That seems to me the most interesting question. In the existentialism of Sartre and Camus, moments of meaning appear suddenly. The feeling of being carried ecstatically away, the feeling that there is meaning in the world. Sartre never actually says in *La Nausee* that these feelings were a mistake. He leaves you to make up your own mind about them. But Sartre's basic position as a Communist later on was that these things are imposed by us on the world. What I'm trying to say is that I don't believe this to be so for a moment. I believe the meaning is really there. The existentialism of Sartre and Camus means in a sense that there's no point in doing anything, if in fact meaning is something you were imposing on reality. In other words, if you are an existentialist of the sort of Sartre and Camus, you would not even set out to do anything. You would just sit there and wonder what there was to do—like Beckett's people in *Waiting for Godot*. Well, I don't feel there's nothing to be done. Essentially for me, I had to start out by disowning these basic tenets of existentialism. That's just the necesary first step as far as I am concerned.

DS: Philosophical novels in England are rare. You seem to be one of the few around noticeably attached to a philosophical system. Has having a philosophical or coherent statement helped you as an artist? Or has it been a distraction?

CW: Well, I don't really see any distinction. I set out thinking along a particular direction, aiming at my own particular goal. Whether I happen to write novels to express my ideas or a volume like *The New Existentialism* makes no difference. As I said in *Religion and the Rebel*, there are certain subtle ideas that can only be expressed in a novel that you simply could not say in a volume on philosophy. Because if you are an existentialist, what you've got to talk about is actual living. As it is, you'll notice that my philosophical books are full of practical examples. Examples, for instance, from the mystics. Always concrete, down-to-earth examples from actual living. So my novels are just in a way extensions of that.

DS: Supernatural phenomena, sexuality, the criminal mind, speculations about the future—all these are predominant interests of yours and indeed of many of your readers, younger ones in particular, to the extent that there seems to have grown up in America a kind of cult around Colin Wilson. How do you react to that?

CW: It's only of interest to me from the point of view that it means people are reading my books and thus I can survive without working quite so hard. I've never been in the least interested in becoming a cult leader. I'm not really a preacher. In *The Outsider*, I said it's tremendously important to work alone, to be capable of standing alone, not to need other people, not to need the applause of other people. I've said in one of my subsequent books that there appears to be what you might call a dominant 5%. The dominant 5% of human beings contains a small percentage who are dominant in quite a different way from the others. A very tiny proportion doesn't need an audience. Such a man is working purely for his own pleasure. I think this to me is the most interesting point—those who genuinely do not need other people, but are totally obsessed by what you might call the impersonal horizon. There are two horizons—the personal and then far beyond that, the impersonal. Most people live and act within the personal horizon.

DS: Many young readers seem to identify with your heroes. What is the chief distinction between your own heroes and the modern heroes we find in today's novels?

CW: It's the old problem which I discuss in *The Age of Defeat*. There is no hero. I mean, most of the modern heroes are sort of oversensitive, miserable people who manage to get themselves killed by the end of the book. The real question is how to create a hero who does something positive. There is this feeling in both Bill Hopkins and myself—this need to create a positive hero. It's interesting that one of the few writers who wrote enthusiastically to Bill after *The Divine and the Decay* came out was Herman Hesse. I think this is because Hesse was doing the same kind of thing in the 1920s and 1930s, and nobody since has been moving in this direction. Also interesting is that I discussed Hesse in *The Outsider* when Hesse had been forgotten in England. I was the first person to write Hesse in English. Apparently there is something by Henry Miller, but I've never seen it. And Hesse's moving in that same direction as Bill is. The *bildungsroman*, the novel about the hero who is looking for something. Hesse never got further than this. All his heroes are looking for something—which is why he is so popular on campuses. But then both Bill and I would like to go beyond this to the hero who actually *does* something, who has found what he's looking for.

INDEX

After Julius (Howard), 14
AMIS, KINGSLEY, American writers, 16-17; "Angry Young Men, 15-16, 51-53; brother-in-law, 14; characterization, 18-19, 25; childhood, 19; class divisions, 21-22, 23, 25; comedy, 18; Dickens, 18; entertainer, 37-38; favorite authors, 13-14; Gardnor House, 13-15; genre fiction, 30; God, 19-20, 28-29; life and fiction, 34-35, 37; man of letters, 40; modernism, 36-37; moralist, 18-19, 20-21, 23-24; on human nature, 17-18; Oxford, 15-16; philistinism, 21; poetry, 29-30; political novel, 16-17; sexuality, 22, 24-25; short fiction, 31; supernatural world, 28-29; travel, 35-36; wife, 14; young writer, 15.
Fiction:
Alteration, The, 33-34.
Anti-Death League, The, 20, 25-30.
Egyptologists, The, 26.
Ending Up, 25, 30-33.
Girl, 20, 25.
Green Man, The, 28-29.
"House on the Headland," 31.
I Like It Here, 21-23, 30, 38.
I Want It Now, 19-20, 26-28.
Jake's Thing, 34-35.
Legacy, The, *39.*
Lucky Jim, 6, 8, 16, 18, 20-23.
One Fat Englishman, 25.
Riverside Villas Murder, The, 25, 30.
Russian Hide and Seek, 14, 38-39.
Take A Girl Like You, 18-19, 22-23.
That Uncertain Feeling, 22, 27-28.
"To See the Sun," 31.
Poetry:
Oxford Book of Light Verse, The, 35.
Amis, Martin, 30.
Animal Farm (Orwell), 16.
Aristotle, 79.
Auden, W. H., 72.

Barth, Karl, 36.
Beckett, Samuel, 91.
Bennett, Arnold, 5.
BRAINE, JOHN, American universities, 58; American writers, 54, 59; "Angry Young Men," 16, 51-52; audience, 53-54, 55; birth, 41; Catholicism, 46, 56; childhood, 46; critics, 55; diary writing, 57-58; education, 41, 46; favorite writers, 41-42; freelance writer, 43; illness, 44; mother, 44, 46; novel writing, 44-45, 46-48; on women, 46-47; politics, 52; Purdue University, 58-59; sexuality, 46-47, 50; short story writing, 45; teaching, 58-59; television, 54; theatre life, 43-44; truthful writer, 50-51; working methods, 57; writer's duty, 53.
Fiction:
"Desert in the Mirror, The," 44.
Fingers of Fire, 56.
Life at the Top, 59.
One and Last Love, 41, 45, 48-49, 54.
Pious Agent, The, 56.
Room at the Top, 41, 44-45, 53, 59.
Stay with Me Till Morning, 50.
Vodi, The, 55-56.
Waiting for Sheila, 48, 50, 59.
Burgess, Anthony, 20, 52.

Camus, Albert, 90-91.
Chesterton, G. K., 5.
Coleridge, Samuel Taylor, 73.
Coming Up For Air (Orwell), 17.
Connolly, Cyril, 5, 46, 54.
Conquest, Robert, 26, 52.

Dickens, Charles, 43, 53.
Donleavy, J. P., 10.
Don't Destroy Me (Hastings), 8-9, 10.
Duras, Marguerite, 51.

Egyptian Book of the Dead, The, 85.
Empson, William, 29.
Enemies of Promise (Connolly), 46.
Entertainer, The (Osborne), 8.

Faust (Goethe), 7.
Ferlinghetti, Laurence, 9.
Fielding, Henry, 10.
Fowles, John, 33, 45.
Fry, Christopher, 5.

Ginger Man (Donleavy), 10.
Ginsberg, Alan, 9, 86.
Goethe, 7.
Greene, Graham, 36.
Gross, John, 39.

Hastings, Michael, 8-9, 10.
Hemingway, Ernest, 5, 10.
Hesse, Hermann, 92.
Holmes, Clellon, 9.
HOPKINS, BILL, "Angry Young Men," 61-62; birth, 61; Britain in the 1950s, 62; education, 61; Marlowe, 66; modern literature, 64; new hero, 10, 64, 65-66; new literature, 65-66; on contemporaries, 62-63.
Fiction:
Divine and the Decay, The, 61, 63 85, 92.

Time and Totality, 63-64.
Howard, Elizabeth Jane, 14.
Huxley, Aldous, 5.

Inadmissable Evidence (Osborne), 8.

James, Henry, 5.
Joyce, James, 5.

Kerouac, Jack, 9, 86.
Kierkegaard, 6.

Larkin, Philip, 37.
Lawrence, D. H., 24-25, 88, 90.
L'Etranger (Camus), 87.
Letters (Barth), 36.
Levin, Bernard, 52.
Look Back in Anger (Osborne), 8, 74-75.
Luther (Osborne), 8.

Mailer, Norman, 5, 16.
Mann, Thomas, 5.
Maugham, Somerset, 34, 62-63, 65.
Middle of the Journey, The, (Trilling), 47-48.
Milton, John, 27, 29.
Milton's God (Empson), 29.
Moby Dick (Melville), 55.
Moon and Sixpence, The, (Maugham), 65.
Mount, Ferdinand, 48-49.
Murdoch, Iris, 6, 8, 16.

Naked and the Dead, The (Mailer), 5, 17.
1984 (Orwell), 17.

O'Hara, John, 54.
On the Pond (Kerouac), 9.
Orton, Joe, 10.
Orwell, George, 16, 17.
Osborne, John, 8, 9, 16, 74-75.
Othello (Shakespeare), 27.

Pinter, Harold, 10.
Pope, Alexander, 73.
Portnoy's Complaint (Roth), 24.
Pound, Ezra, 5.
Powell, Anthony, 52.
Priestly, J. B., 6, 8, 44.
Proust, Marcel, 87.

Razor's Edge, The (Maugham), 65.
Rexroth, 9.
Rise and Fall of the Man of Letters, The (Gross), 39.
Robbe-Grillet, 51.
Robbers, The (Schuller), 7.
Roth, Philip, 24.

Salinger, J. D., 17.
Sartre, Jean-Paul, 90-91.
Saturday Night and Sunday Morning (Sillitoe), 10.
Schuller, 7.
Senior Commoner, The, 39.
Shaw, George Bernard, 5.
Sidney, Sir Philip, 37.
Sillitoe, Alan, 10.
Smollett, Henry, 5.
Stoppard, Tom, 10.
Tom Jones (Fielding), 10.
Trilling, Lionel, 47-48.
Tynan, Kenneth, 8.

WAIN, JOHN, "Angry Young Men," 15, 74-75; audience, 75-76; Coleman, 76-77; conception of literature, 73-74; Cushman, 80; education, 67; jazz, 76-77; literary criticism, 70-71; motivation, 81-82; Oxford, 68; poetry, 71-73, 80-81; university career, 69; Wales, 78; wife, 78; writer's career, 69-70; writing methods, 80-81.
Fiction:
Frank, 81.
Hurry on Down, 5-6, 8, 16, 67.
Pardoner's Tale, The, 78-79.
Smaller Sky, The, 77.
Strike the Father Dead, 76-77.
Winter in the Hills, A, 78.
Young Visitors, The, 77-78.
Nonfiction:
Samuel Johnson, 79-80.
Waiting for Godot (Beckett), 91.
Waugh, Evelyn, 36.
Wells, H. G., 5.
Whitman, Walt, 90.
Wilson, Angus, 5.
WILSON, COLIN, "Angry Young Men," 16, 84; audience, 92; brain experiments, 89; career, 83-84; Cornwall, 84; existentialism, 90-91; horsewhipping story, 86; influences, 7, 84-85; moments of joy, 87-88; philosophical novel, 91-92; publicity, 86; revolution in consciousness, 88; wife, 86-87.
Fiction:
Black Room, The, 89-90.
Mind Parasites, The, 88.
Ritual in the Dark, The, 84-85.
Sex Diary of Gerard Sorme, The, 88.
Nonfiction:
Age of Defeat, The, 92.
Beyond the Outsider, 87.
Mysteries, 87.
New Existentialism, The, 91.
Occult, The, 84.
Origins of the Sexual Impulse, 87.
Outsider, The, 6-7, 82-85, 88, 92.
Religion and the Rebel, 7, 9, 83, 87, 91.
Stature of Man, The, 87.
Strength to Dream, The, 87.
Wodehouse, P. G., 9, 37-38.
Woolf, Virginia, 54-55.
Wordsworth, William, 73.